THE SCOTT AND LAURIE OKI SERIES

IN ASIAN AMERICAN STUDIES

THE SCOTT AND LAURIE OKI SERIES

IN ASIAN AMERICAN STUDIES

BORN IN SEATTLE

The Campaign for Japanese American Redress

ROBERT SADAMU SHIMABUKURO

UNIVERSITY OF WASHINGTON PRESS
Seattle and London

This book is published with the assistance of a grant
from the Scott and Laurie Oki Endowed Fund
for the publication of Asian American studies.

This project was made possible by the
Civil Liberties Public Education Fund,
the National JACL Legacy Fund,
the Seattle Chapter Japanese American Citizens League,
the Minoru Masuda Memorial Fund,
and the Washington Coalition on Redress.

Library of Congress Cataloging-in-Publication Data
Shimabukuro, Robert Sadamu.
Born in Seattle : the campaign for Japanese American redress /
Robert Sadamu Shimabukuro.
p. cm. — (The Scott and Laurie Oki series in Asian American studies)
Includes bibliographical references and index.
ISBN 0-295-98142-3 (alk. paper)
1. World War, 1939–1945—Reparations.
2. World War, 1939–1945—United States.
3. Japanese Americans—Evacuation and relocation, 1942–1945.
4. Japanese Americans—Civil rights.
I. Title. II. Series.
D819.U6 S45 2001 2001027170

The paper used in this publication is acid-free and recycled from 10 percent post-
consumer and at least 50 percent pre-consumer waste. It meets the minimum
requirements of American National Standard for Information Sciences—
Permanence of Paper for Printed Library Materials, ANSI z39.48–1984. ⊗ ♻

redress—(rē-dres', ri-dres'; v. ri-dres'), *n.* 1. the setting right of what is wrong: *redress of abuses.* 2. relief from wrong or injury. 3. compensation or satisfaction for a wrong or injury.—*vt.* 4. to set right; remedy or repair (wrongs, injuries, etc.). 5. to correct or reform (abuses, evils, etc.). 6. to remedy or relieve (suffering, want, etc.). 7. to adjust evenly again, as a balance.
—*Random House Compact Unabridged Dictionary,* 1996

The case is clear, the cause is just,
and the time for action is long overdue.
—Dr. Minoru Masuda, as quoted in the Washington State
Legislature by Rep. Art Wang on May 6, 1983

While the national drive is relatively recognized and documented,
little is as yet known about the initial efforts of the movement,
in which Seattle played a key role.
—Yasuko I. Takezawa, *Breaking the Silence:
Redress and Japanese American Ethnicity*

History demands that the person who gave birth to an idea
must be recognized when it reaches maturation.
—Washington State Supreme Court Justice Charles Z. Smith,
interviewed on November 15, 1997

CONTENTS

FOREWORD

On August 10, 1988, the day President Ronald Reagan signed the Civil Liberties Act, a TV reporter asked me, "How does it feel to beat City Hall?" We were all rather dazed by our victory, and I hardly knew how to answer. Up to that point, I had rarely thought deeply about the true nature of the struggle for redress for the Japanese Americans who had been incarcerated during World War II. We had been moving along step by step, bit by bit. Even though the internment had taken place more than 40 years before, this fight just felt like the right thing to do, to rally behind and to pursue, win or lose. And so, by focusing on the details, one could ignore the quixotic, visionary, almost fool-hardy dimensions of trying to get the United States government to apologize for and to redress those wrongs that, to many, seemed a lifetime ago.

Redress was a truly monumental achievement. Even today, our lofty democratic ideals remain illusory goals that are too often trampled in the hurly-burly rush of history. The road to justice is littered with land mines triggered by human weakness, prejudice, cowardice, and, in the case of the redress campaign, some people's need to keep pure the reputations of our national leaders.

Good intentions and wishes are not enough to impel people to action. Redress remained an elusive dream for many even while it seemed necessary for a closure of some kind, a healing for a population that had undergone the outrages of incarceration, the loss of a lifetime of work, and the tearing out of roots that had just begun to take hold in their communities. In fact, our apparent lack of anger and the hard work we put into rebuilding our lives had only earned us rather pejorative labels: we were the "quiet Americans" and, later, the "model minority." But anger, resentment, and feelings of having been victimized were still present. No one had forgotten the past, but, in spite of the occasional lone exhortative voice, redress seemed an impossible fantasy.

So how did we get from hopelessness to the halls of Congress and the Supreme Court, right up to the president's desk? Redress is an amazing story, and Washington State played a major role in getting the idea out of the clouds and down to earth, before the American people. Like every other story, this is also the story of individuals, of a coming together of many elements, planned and unplanned, that combined to gather the momentum to bring about a successful conclusion. And that conclusion was no isolated victory for a small minority group whose political clout was minuscule. Rather, it was the result of many voices, many factions, rallying: of getting the country to "do the right thing."

Think of those who played large roles in the tale: Mike Lowry, an Irish American; Gary Locke and Art Wang, Chinese Americans; George Fleming, Ron Sims, and Charles Z. Smith, African Americans; Dolores Sibonga and Frankie Irigon, Filipino Americans; Charles Royer and James Dolliver, Euroamericans. This multicultural network of support was made up of individuals who, along with hundreds of others, contributed crucial parts at particular junctures.

To keep the struggle alive was vital in the beginning, and the fact that it was kept alive is due to a staunch, dedicated individual, Henry Miyatake, who vowed to go down fighting, and to a band of dedicated Seattle activists, including Cherry Kinoshita, Chuck Kato, Ken Nakano, Mike Nakata, and Shosuke Sasaki, who proved the "quiet American" myth to be a lie.

In part, we can also credit the national mood. The raising of public consciousness during the sixties and seventies, through national civil rights battles and protests against the Vietnam War, created a climate that encouraged our questioning the past, reexamining our collective experience. We'd like to think that justice triumphs, but in the course of life we know that injustice is equally likely to win, usually by outlasting the forces for a better outcome. The inertia that has to be overcome is tremendous. But there is always the possibility, the hope, that good things will happen if stout-hearted individuals are willing to stick their necks out and take the lead.

Washington's story is a special story. In our little community, in this Pacific Coast state of the union, it is thrilling to know that we had the visionaries and the planners, those willing to take a chance, and that they were able to continue with the support of the population. We were instrumental in getting the movement going, constantly pushing it along, and, finally, insisting that redress become part of the national agenda. We can speculate endlessly on why the movement began here and in this way. Perhaps the social and political climate here is more cohesive and yet more open than in other states; perhaps the possibilities are greater. For whatever reason, it happened, and we now know that we can make change happen. And so the bigger story is that redress is a triumph for all Americans, giving us the heart to pursue other ideals. A few more years may need to pass before we understand how unusual and symbolic this win actually was. The historical relevance and the sweetness of redress become all the more apparent as we turn to study the evolution of this movement as it began to unfold.

CHIZU OMORI
Seattle, Washington
July 2000

PREFACE

Learning about Pain and Triumph

In early 1979, I received a call from Peggy Nagae, a Portland, Oregon, civil rights attorney. She was co-chair of the Portland Day of Remembrance, a day to commemorate Executive Order 9066, and she was looking for people who would be willing to help organize the event.

"I asked my secretary, Susan Williams, if she knew any activist-type Japanese Americans," Peggy explained, "and she gave me your name. I wonder if you'd be interested in coming to a planning meeting."

I hesitated because I knew next to nothing about Executive Order 9066 and the experience of Japanese Americans during World War II. Born and raised in Hawaii, I would never have heard of the concentration camps had it not been for the rumors that our junior high school band teacher had spent time in the "camps." In the late 1960s, just out of college and homesick, I had wandered into the Portland City Library and picked out a book solely because of its title, *Hawaii: End of the Rainbow*.[1] Written by Kazuo Miyamoto, the novel chronicles two generations (Issei and Nisei) of a Japanese American family in Hawaii, from the early immigration through the end of World War II. What was striking were the descriptions of "camp life." A central character in the novel had been shipped to the mainland; another was studying on the West Coast when President Franklin Delano Roosevelt issued Executive Order 9066. It was my first awareness that Americans of Japanese ancestry from Hawaii had been hauled off to these concentration camps. Miyamoto's recounting revealed only some of the horror of the camps, but it did serve to keep me from being totally ignorant about the experience.

I gave Peggy a hesitant yes and attended the next meeting. I was seated next to Dr. Homer Yasui. Frank Chin, Frank Abe, and Kathy Wong were talking about the upcoming event. Chin was giving a "how to handle the media" workshop. I was trying to figure out how I could be of help when I didn't know a thing. I turned to Homer and asked tentatively, "You know any good books I can read to find out more about this stuff?"

To Homer's credit, he didn't start chastising me for being "a Sansei ignoramus" (as someone else had earlier called me) or, even worse, "a Hawaiian Sansei ignoramus" (as others later called me). Instead, he answered, "As a matter of fact, I do." And he proceeded to pull out a long list from his stack of papers. "Here," he said, "these ought to help you."

I skipped out of the workshop, thinking there was no way this group would or should let me speak to the media, and headed to the library, where I checked out the first book on Homer's list, Michi Weglyn's *Years of Infamy*.

I took it home and thumbed through it. The first photo: two children who looked like my cousins, accompanying an elderly woman, perhaps a grandmother, all with what looked like baggage-claim tags attached to their clothing. The caption read, "Most of the 110,000 persons removed for reasons of 'national security' were school-age children, infants and young adults not yet of voting age."[2]

Estelle Ishigo's drawings of toilets and showers followed, as did newspaper clippings about "riots" in the camps. Next came 300-plus pages of text and documents describing the events leading up to and resulting from Executive Order 9066, its legislative corollary Public Law 503, and all the proclamations that "justified" corralling and incarcerating more than 120,000 persons of Japanese ancestry "on a record which wouldn't support a conviction for stealing a dog."[3]

I read Weglyn's book in one long sitting, taking time to eat, maybe to nap a bit. It was an intensely emotional weekend. I was angry, bewildered, anguished, sad. And the two kids wearing the baggage-claim tags haunted me. The weekend passed. I told Homer Yasui I couldn't read anything else on his list for now. It would drive me nuts. Emotional overload. Too much pain.

I told Peggy I would help, but in a limited capacity until I had a better understanding of what had happened. I would need to learn more. To my surprise, Peggy answered, "I'm learning, too. My parents never told me anything about their experience."

That conversation took place more than 20 years ago. I haven't stopped learning.

Working on redress in Portland, I needed to acquaint myself with the expulsion and imprisonment of civilians, mostly of Japanese ancestry, during World War II. When the congressional Commission on Wartime Relocation and

Internment of Civilians (CWRIC) held its hearings in Seattle in 1981, Peggy asked me to help internees write their testimony. I heard about the losses and the crippling effects of the incarceration from those who had experienced it. It was like pulling teeth. Japanese Americans in Portland were still rather reluctant to talk about their experiences. Some, after working so hard to write their testimony, decided not to testify, finding the process overwhelming or intimidating.

Over the next decade I was to learn a lot more, from people who needed a voice but were reluctant to tell their stories, and from research necessitated by work on a range of projects: reversal of the Supreme Court's conviction of Minoru Yasui, who had challenged the 1942 curfew law; a year and a half of editing *Pacific Citizen,* the newspaper of the Japanese American Citizens League (JACL); and, with hundreds of volunteers who had developed into community historians, the production of *Executive Order 9066: 50 Years Before and 50 Years After,* a groundbreaking 1992 exhibition for Seattle's Wing Luke Asian Museum, on the history of the Japanese American community in the Puget Sound area.

An encounter that occurred during the period of this exhibition made me realize how deep the scars of the incarceration were. The exhibit was drawing national attention. There had been a lot of publicity generated about it, and a Nisei woman who knew I had been working on it began telling me about her experiences.

"You know, Bob," she said, "I would like to see the exhibit, but I just can't. Everyone says it's a good exhibit, but it brought back the bad memories. That's why I don't want to see it. I just don't want to go through that experience again. Especially with the general public being there, too."

"Well," I replied, "if you want a personal tour, no one around, just your friends, I can arrange one. Maybe on a Sunday, after hours. I'd be very interested in your comments about the exhibit."

She answered with a shrug and a "maybe." I told her to give me a call if she wanted a tour.

Our paths crossed often during that time, and a few weeks later I heard her calling me.

"Hey, Bob! Wait a minute! I wanted to tell you I'm really angry at you! You ruined a perfectly good day!"

Uh-oh, I said to myself—it was difficult to judge whether she was joking. "What happened?"

"You remember last Sunday, how beautiful it was? Well, I thought maybe this was a perfect time to go see the exhibit. I was feeling real good. The flowers were blooming. It was so nice. So I went."

"And?" I was a bit wary: her tone indicated a tragedy of some sort.

"The beginning was okay. The immigration. The family and community things. But then all the pictures, the newspaper articles, started to get me. The stuff about 'Japs.' Humiliating. Again. My legs were shaking. I continued and turned the corner, and there was the barrack scene you did. It was too much. I couldn't go on. I just broke down." Tears came to her eyes as she completed her report on the exhibition. "A nice man helped me past the rest of the exhibit, and I got to a bench and sat there for the longest time. I left the museum and here was this beautiful day outside, but I couldn't appreciate it. You ruined it."

I was overwhelmed. "I'm sorry to hear that. I'm sorry for recommending the exhibit at all," I apologized, with an embarrassed smile.

She also smiled, through her tears, but it was obvious she was still holding me responsible for bringing up memories and emotions she had long suppressed. And there was no doubt in my mind that suppressing those memories had been essential to her survival. This brief conversation, more than any books or photographs, deeply and vividly imprinted on me the effects of the incarceration on the Japanese American population.

What I learned from history books was basic Asian American history: that Executive Order 9066 and the war years were not the beginning of discrimination against Japanese Americans; that anti-Asian / anti-Japanese laws and attitudes had been established long before the bombing of Pearl Harbor; that state and federal laws barring immigration, citizenship, land ownership, marriage (to whites), and access to certain areas of housing and employment were a common part of the landscape.[4] I learned that, in spite of these laws, thriving Japanese American communities, with businesses, schools, cultural organizations, and newspapers, were created in urban and rural areas, only to be destroyed by governmental edicts and laws during World War II. These laws also produced lasting and crippling divisions within the Japanese American community, which today still bears the scars of war-era disagreements about how to respond to laws and regulations such as Public Law 503, Executive Order 9066, "loyalty" questionnaires, and the military draft.

In order to write this book, I turned to the participants themselves to learn history—this time to record a triumph. I learned about the redress activists, expert community organizers, among them thinkers and planners, writers, political analysts, and grassroots lobbyists, who led the campaign to redress an outrageous act committed by their own government. What follows is the story, spanning more than 20 years, of the Seattle activists who pursued legislative redress for the violation of their constitutional rights that had been carried out through Executive Order 9066 and Public Law 503. All Americans owe a great debt to the activists who worked to achieve redress.

The first apologies and payments were issued in 1990, but stirrings for redress had begun in the late 1960s and early 1970s with Edison Uno, in San Francisco, and Henry Miyatake, in Seattle. (Uno and Miyatake began their quests separately, but Miyatake found Seattle more receptive to his proposals than Uno found San Francisco to his.) This account is in no way intended as a definitive history of the redress movement. It is a story about the often neglected contributions of the Seattle community to the passage of the Civil Liberties Act of 1988, and it covers Seattle redress activities from the late 1960s to the early 1990s. Nor does it intend to minimize the work of others, who have contributed so much to the successful pursuit of legislative redress: the national Japanese American Citizens League and its Legislative Education Committee (LEC), the organization's lobbying arm; the attorneys and support committees who fought to reverse the Supreme Court decisions in the Korematsu, Hirabayashi, and Yasui cases; the National Council for Japanese American Redress, and its $27 billion suit against the United States for its violations of constitutional rights; and the National Coalition for Redress / Reparations.

It should be noted that two successful campaigns—one for the repeal, in 1971, of Title II of the Internal Security Act of 1950 (also called the Emergency Detention Act), and the other for the 1977 pardon by President Gerald Ford of Iva Toguri d'Acquino—bolstered the confidence of this country's relatively small Japanese American population in its ability to affect public policy at the national level. Although they lie outside the scope of the present work, these campaigns also played a role in the redress movement.

R.S.S.

July 2000

ACKNOWLEDGMENTS

A book is rarely produced without the help of many, and this book is no exception. I would like to thank the funders of this project: the Civil Liberties Public Education Fund, the National JACL Legacy Fund, the Seattle Chapter Japanese American Citizens League, the Minoru Masuda Memorial Fund, and the Washington Coalition on Redress.

Thanks and appreciation are also due to members of the Seattle Redress Project, who provided impetus, research materials, time for interviews, advice, and some of the writing of this book: Frank Abe, Tetsuden Kashima, Henry Miyatake, Mako Nakagawa, Ken Nakano, Chizu Omori, Roger Shimizu, Sam Shoji, and co-chairs Chuck Kato and Cherry Kinoshita.

Personal interviews played an important part in the research of this book, and I appreciate those who gave me their time: Frank Chin, James Dolliver, George Fleming, Gordon Hirabayashi, Aki Kurose, Gary Locke, Mike Lowry, Mich Matsudaira, Tomio Moriguchi, Ben Nakagawa, Mike Nakata, Kaz Oshiki, Karen Seriguchi, Ron Sims, Charles Z. Smith, Calvin Takagi, John Tateishi, Jim Tsujimura, Clifford Uyeda, T. J. Vassar, and Ruth Woo.

Unless otherwise noted, all information and quotations from Seattle Redress Project activists—Chuck Kato, Cherry Kinoshita, Mich Matsudaira, Henry Miyatake, Tomio Moriguchi, Mako Nakagawa, Mike Nakata, Ken Nakano, and Sam Shoji—are from personal interviews with the author.

I would also like to acknowledge the assistance of the researchers, transcribers, and reviewers: Wayne Au, Ron Chew, Aiko Yoshinaga Herzig, Meredith Higashi, Lane Hirabayashi, William Hohri, Tom Ikeda, Tosh and Aki Ito, Alice Ito, Ruthann Kurose, Alan Lau, Ron Mamiya, Mike Nakata, Tim Otani, Karen Seriguchi, Beth Takekawa, Yasuko Takezawa, Mayumi Tsutakawa, Vicki Toyohara-Mukai, Homer and Miyuki Yasui, and Lynn Yoshioka.

Finally, much gratitude and appreciation are due Mira Chieko Shimabukuro for her valuable writing assistance in tying together the often disparate parts of the book.

BORN IN SEATTLE

The Campaign for Japanese American Redress

1 / Awakening

Though to all outward appearance the recovery of Japanese Americans has been good to remarkable, the rejection and social isolation of the war years have left scars which have not entirely disappeared. A bitter evacuation legacy shared by ex-inmates in varying degrees is a psychic damage which the Nisei describe as "castration": a deep consciousness of personal inferiority, a proclivity to noncommunication and inarticulateness, evidenced in a shying away from exposure which might subject them to further hurt. . . . The more militant, usually younger, Nisei agree that it's high time to get out from under the debilitating "quiet American" label if their needs are to be taken seriously.

—Michi Weglyn[1]

1967–68: HIGH TIME

"What's with you, anyway?" Mike Nakata asked Henry Miyatake. "You don't behave like a 'normal' Nikkei."[2]

"What do you mean?"

"I liked the way you did your presentation. You didn't shrink away from those guys. Answered their questions. Handled the give-and-take. You didn't back down."

Miyatake and Nakata, both Boeing engineers, had just come from a Supersonic Transport (SST) program meeting. They were the only nonmanagers in this group, but their expertise was needed: Miyatake's in integrating government regulations and commercial requirements, Nakata's in welding processes. Miyatake had been impressed by Nakata's contribution in these weekly meetings; he was pleased that Nakata was now impressed with his. Miyatake had worked at Boeing for nine years; Nakata, for twelve. Both noticed that the *hakujin* (white) managers never seemed to give Nisei engineers their due credit. Education and ingenuity should command respect, not scorn.

The Nisei engineers, Miyatake decided, were seen as too polite, too kind, too soft, almost "castrated."

"We take a lot of crap without answering back, and we're always reticent about showing our capabilities," the two engineers reasoned.

Not enough self-confidence. The managers knew it and exploited it. In observing the dynamics of these meetings of management staff, both saw in each other what they wanted to see in themselves—the ability and willingness to defend their views.

Nakata was sure that the World War II incarceration of Japanese Americans was a major cause of Nisei lack of self-confidence and their managers' scorn.

"We got taken for a ride," he said. "Our bank accounts were disrupted. We got wiped out economically. Got put away. We didn't do anything. All *hakujin* feel like they can walk all over us, without us making a noise."

Miyatake agreed with Nakata and was convinced that something had to be done to erase these perceptions of the Nikkei in America and to regain the respect and sense of self-worth that many had lost during the wartime expulsion and incarceration.[3]

JAPANESE AMERICAN PRIDE AND SHAME: AN EXHIBIT

[*Pride and Shame*] was the first time we in the larger community had an opportunity to see . . . through this very professional and elaborate photographic exhibit . . . what actually happened. This was, I think, the beginning of a conscious awareness. Especially of non-Asians. But [also] many Asians. The younger generations of Asian / Japanese [Americans] were not fully aware of what happened during the Second World War. And this was the beginning of a new awareness.
—The Hon. Charles Z. Smith, Washington State Supreme Court Justice[4]

In early 1970, Tomio Moriguchi, by education a young mechanical engineer, and by occupation the owner of Uwajimaya, a thriving Asian food and import store, received a call from the Museum of History and Industry (MOHAI), in Seattle, asking for help with an exhibition being planned for the summer. The museum had scheduled a three-month exhibit related to Japan, commemorating Expo '70, in Osaka, and wanted to know if Moriguchi, chair of the Seattle Chapter Japanese American Citizens League (JACL) Cultural Committee, was interested in participating in the planning of the exhibit.

Seeing a great opportunity to involve younger Japanese Americans in a JACL-sponsored event, Moriguchi agreed, with the understanding that the exhibit would be about local Japanese American history and activities. The budget was $600: $200 each from the Seattle Chapter JACL, the Japanese Cultural Festival Committee, and the museum.

As Moriguchi and the Seattle Chapter JACL Youth Committee began to collect photographs, cultural objects, and other artifacts, other community members—representing the Nisei Veterans Committee, the Boy Scouts, the Rokka Ski Club, and the Asian Coalition for Equality (a group of Asian American educators concerned with civil rights)—all expressed interest in working on the exhibit.

Individuals also volunteered their time. Larry Matsuda, a school teacher, donated photos and memorabilia collected by his parents. Roy Tsuboi, a photographer, had just started his arts and graphics shop and had the equipment to prepare all the photographs for presentation by the museum. Frank Fujii, an artist, helped with the graphics, and Harold Kawaguchi led a crew in constructing a full-scale mock-up of the interior of a typical concentration-camp barracks. Dr. Joe Okimoto, Kathy Miyamoto, Elaine Aoki, Sharon Fujii, Jiro Namatame, and Karen Tsukiji also worked on the exhibit.

Japanese American Pride and Shame opened July 7, 1970, ran until September 30, and was viewed by more than 34,000 people. Viewers saw artifacts and photographs that told a compressed history of Japanese Americans in the Northwest. Included were photos of Issei railroad, dairy, and cannery workers, the Nisei 442nd Regimental Combat Team, community honor rolls, and even a poem written by a Sansei. But the exhibit also included examples of the struggles faced by the community, embodied by early Yellow Peril editorial cartoons, the text of Executive Order 9066, and photos of the expulsion and incarceration in addition to contemporary racist headlines alluding to the return of the Yellow Peril.

For a group previously reluctant to speak publicly about the expulsion, the community's participation was surprising. But many people who had experienced camp life felt, like Roy Tsuboi, that they "had a story to tell."

Because each subcommittee was made responsible for a certain aspect of the exhibit, things did not always go smoothly, according to Tsuboi; however, differences dissipated as a friendly competition developed between church and community groups and their respective sections.

"The only conflict we had with the exhibit was with the MOHAI director, Sutton Gustison, who complained about the anti-Japanese and internment stuff," said Tomio Moriguchi. "I guess she didn't like history that wasn't kind." Moriguchi said later that the community interest in planning and building the exhibit was not something he had expected: "Maybe the timing was right. It gave people an opportunity to release some pent-up emotions, feelings that were bottled up. The churches didn't feel redress was their bag. But the project was also an opportunity for people to mix, to have a good time working on something. There was an awareness [about redress] just starting."[5]

"AMERICAN DEMOCRACY: WHAT IT MEANS TO ME"

Up until high school I was a conscientious student. I guess I would have been a completely different person had I not gone to camp. Maybe I would have been something worthwhile.

—Henry Miyatake[6]

On February 19, 1942, President Franklin Delano Roosevelt signed Executive Order 9066, setting the stage for the federal government's removal of all individuals of Japanese ancestry from designated military zones encompassing the entire West Coast.[7] Henry Miyatake was twelve years old when he and his family were first sent to the animal stalls on the Puyallup fairgrounds, infamously known as Camp Harmony. From there, the Miyatakes, along with 7,200 other Japanese Americans, would be taken by train to Minidoka, Idaho. No one knew when, or if, they would ever be free again. Most would be incarcerated for the next two to four years.[8]

After completing his freshman year at Minidoka's Hunt High School, Miyatake calculated that he would be able to graduate during his junior year because by then he would have been able to gather the required credits. He looked forward to graduating early, since he wanted, as he put it later, "to get the heck out of that dumb high school," where strict rules had been instituted on absences and grades.

"If you got one F in one class, you got all F's for all the classes," Miyatake explained later. This rule would have a huge impact on him.

As juniors, students were required to take a class in civics, which required them to write a term paper on everything they had learned. The previous year, Miyatake had been selected to be on the reception committee for the visiting Truman Anti-American Investigation Committee. As he recalled:

> The school representatives were assigned to greet [Truman's committee] and planned to give them a tour of the high school. Well, those son-of-a-guns never showed up. . . . Consequently, in the congressional record, they made a Truman Investigation Committee report. And I spent my ten cents getting a copy of that dumb thing. . . . I couldn't believe what the hell they wrote. They said that they had been to five different camps. Minidoka was one of them, and they [the camp] . . . laid out, on the dining room table, linen, silverware, food served by waitresses, and all this kind of crap. I just couldn't believe that report. . . . I thought to myself, Well, dammit, if this [is] an American democracy, then we're in deep doo-doo. So my term paper was called "American Democracy: What It Means To Me." . . . It was all the anger, frustration, and all the things about American society like the treatment of Blacks, and Indians and . . . the treatment against Orientals, Chinese in particular, and ourselves. . . . Miss Ammerman wouldn't accept the paper. She said, "I can't accept it. This is not civics. It's not the kind of material that I'm going to accept." So I said, "Well, I'm going to exercise one of my constitutional rights, and that's the freedom of the press. And I'm going to stand by it." . . . They failed me in her class, and I got F's for all the other classes. So [they] automatically booted me out of the school. And that was the end of it. . . . I was fifteen when I got thrown out. I would have been sixteen and graduated.[9]

Asked how this experience had affected him in the long run, Miyatake responded simply, "It really screwed me up. . . . I spent a lot of time writing that paper. It was eight years until I was able to continue my formal education process." And he pointed out that he was not the only one who got kicked out of school because of camp policies:

> The most unfortunate part . . . was the fact that . . . during this time period, we were very impressionable students. . . . It was a turning point for students that were wavering, and they were put over the cliff. . . . [Those school policies] caused so much mental prohibitions—psychological, economic,

and educational—that they just never came back. And I think this is the
biggest loss that we never talk about.[10]

THE CHALLENGE

In 1968, after Miyatake repeatedly questioned his attorney and friend, Anthony
Hoare, about constitutional law and the World War II incarceration, Hoare
challenged him. Giving him a book about *ex parte Milligan*,[11] and another
titled *How to Find the Law*,[12] along with a pass to the University of Washington
Law School library, Hoare said, "If you're really interested, then you should
do your research." Hoare also introduced Miyatake to Arval Morris, a
University of Washington legal scholar and professor who, along with Hoare,
became Miyatake's early legal mentor.

Between 1968 and 1974, Miyatake spent much of his spare time at the UW
law library. It was during a data search there that Miyatake found *Prejudice,
War, and the Constitution*,[13] a book that opened his eyes to possibilities. "The
more I looked at the book, the more interested I became [in] some of the
things that might possibly be done," he would later say. "It's a classic book
on the evacuation and constitutional issues." Most important, *Prejudice, War,
and the Constitution* also suggested some possible remedies.

Two courses were open. The legislative course would mean petitioning
Congress for redress. The judicial course would mean trying to get a court
case heard before the Supreme Court so that forced expulsion would be
declared unconstitutional. At first, Arval Morris advised against the judicial
approach. He contended that, because the statute of limitations had run out
on the expulsion, it would be expensive and nearly impossible to have the
Supreme Court hear the case. A judicial approach could be taken if new evidence were found that could get around the statute of limitations. Or,
because the logic of expulsion said that Nikkei were guilty of being a "military threat" precisely and only because they were of Japanese ancestry, it might
be possible to tie the case to similar current cases that dealt with the issue of
guilt by association.

At that time, according to Miyatake, one of the strongest "guilt by association" cases was against the Black Panther Party, which was being charged
with general conspiracy to overthrow the United States government. The
charge was brought, not against individual members, but rather against the
entire party; in other words, all Black Panthers would be deemed guilty precisely because they were Black Panthers. Because of the far-reaching impact

of a conspiracy charge, Morris believed there was a good possibility that the case would reach the Supreme Court. If Japanese Americans incarcerated during World War II tagged along on the Black Panthers' case, Morris reasoned, a ruling on the wartime expulsion might result.[14]

Morris advised Miyatake to find all the similarities between the Black Panthers and Japanese Americans. He told him to find the full description of what the government was saying about the Panthers, as well as what the government said about Fred Korematsu and Gordon Hirabayashi, the Japanese American defendants in two test cases regarding the constitutionality of Executive Order 9066 and Public Law 503. Morris also suggested investigating what had caused the government to go after the Panthers (exactly what the Panthers had allegedly done) and, likewise, exactly what the Japanese Americans had allegedly done.

Miyatake found himself in a peculiar position. The Japanese American community was none too thrilled about this idea. "What are you doing?" Nisei attorneys and community leaders asked him. "We don't want to be associated with the Panthers!" But Morris, convinced that the Black Panther case was going to reach the Supreme Court, thought this would be the quickest way to get a ruling on the expulsion, and Miyatake was attracted by the idea of a quick ruling. However, according to Miyatake, the U.S. government dropped the Panther case while it was in the Ninth Circuit Court of Appeals.

Miyatake had mixed emotions over the time he had spent researching the matter: on the one hand, he was sad that a ruling would not come soon; on the other, community attitudes would probably have prevented him from actually carrying out the plan.

Morris, Miyatake recalls, then offered this advice regarding a court case, or finding new evidence and then suing the government: "Unless you have a half-million to three-quarters of a million dollars to throw away, you will never be able to get it to the Supreme Court. That's how much money it would take. Going through Congress, you got a good chance on the constitutional issue. It will take a long time. You gotta organize a lot of people. It involves a lot of hard work. But you got a good chance."

With those words, Miyatake turned his attention to redress legislation, and he began a long road of research on exactly what it would take to pass a bill to compensate Japanese Americans for the World War II expulsion and incarceration. He found that Morris was right: redress would take a lot of people and a lot of hard work.[15]

PRIDE AND SHAME ON TOUR

After seeing *Pride and Shame* at the Museum of History and Industry, Kenneth Hopkins, director of the Washington State Capitol Museum, approached Tomio Moriguchi. He wanted to apply to the National Endowment for the Humanities (NEH) for a grant to fund a joint museum-community project: making *Pride and Shame* an exhibit that would tour the Northwest. Moriguchi referred Hopkins to Dr. Minoru Masuda, professor of psychiatry at the University of Washington. Moriguchi felt that Masuda was more familiar with grantsmanship and would therefore be better suited to assist the museum director.

With Hopkins's encouragement, Masuda and Don Kazama, a local social worker, started gathering volunteers to modify the exhibit into a traveling history book. Masuda was interested in the exhibit, according to Moriguchi, because he saw the community's interest in telling its story as a very encouraging sign of Japanese American awakening and self-consciousness. As Masuda wrote in the grant proposal, "We know that one of the most effective ways to deal with history is to relate it in terms of individuals who lived it. Personal experience is the foundation of history. It is also real and meaningful to the non-academician who comprises the public majority."[16] In addition to the exhibit itself, Masuda proposed panel discussions with people who had experienced the imprisonment.

The proposal, which included a request for $8,571, was mailed to the NEH in late October 1970. In late March 1971, Hopkins received the letter from the NEH that all of them had been waiting for: the exhibit organizers had been awarded just over $6,500 in support of the project, under Masuda's direction.

Although the grant covered the project from July 1, 1971, to July 30, 1972, planning had begun almost immediately after the end of the MOHAI exhibit. Key participants in the early planning, besides Moriguchi, Kazama, and Masuda, were Harold Kawaguchi, in charge of exhibit design; Jim Morishima, Fran Wada, and Ben Yorita, in charge of the training manual for presenters; and Calvin Takagi, the training coordinator, responsible for recruiting "knowledgeable and articulate people" who would serve on the panels in the areas to which the exhibit traveled.[17]

This early-planning committee recruited people who would be willing to serve on the panels and to edit, revise, build, and install the exhibit as it toured. It was at this time that Frank Fujii designed the logo that is still being used today as the "call to arms" in the Nikkei community. Fujii's logo—a graphic

design representing the *ichi, ni,* and *san* generations (Issei, Nisei, Sansei) sur-
rounded by a circle—and its subsequent revisions (the circle was later wound
with barbed wire) were to become synonymous with redress as groups
around the country adopted the logo as their own.[18]

Because of the exhibit's success, Masuda applied for an extension of the
program in 1972, asking the NEH for funds to cover another two years. By
1975, the range of people who had seen the exhibit included students from
high schools, colleges, and universities; teachers in various workshops; members of church groups; political activists; and the general public at the
Western Washington Fair in Puyallup, site of the former Camp Harmony.
The last traveling presentation was in early 1975 at Western Washington State
College, in Bellingham, although the exhibit was brought out for Days of
Remembrance and other community events for several years afterward. Well
over 100,000 people had seen the exhibit during its tour.[19]

The response was largely positive, according to Masuda's reports to the
NEH, and according to Calvin Takagi, who moderated many of the panel discussions. As Takagi later said, however, "We had one experience at Sam-
mamish High School in Bellevue that was not very good." He explained:

> Some of the questions from the audience were kind of hostile. . . . One stu-
> dent, after we had talked about being interned, said, "You guys ever been over
> to Yakima?" and I said, "Yeah, so?" and he said, "Well, I've seen the farm labor
> camps over there and what terrible conditions those people live in over there,
> and it sounds to me like where you were was a lot better than that." I said, "I
> don't care whether you're living in a flush housing with gold-plated faucets:
> if you're in prison, the thing that you're lacking most is freedom." That soured
> me. That one thing stuck out in my mind. But also at the same school, after
> the thing was over, there was this Nisei woman who worked in the office, and
> she came up to us, and she said she was really glad we came over because her
> son was in school and he didn't know anything about this stuff.[20]

The *Pride and Shame* exhibit was the community's first step toward
exposing what most felt to be a painful personal experience very rarely displayed to their own children, let alone to the general public. A pool of speakers willing and able to talk about their World War II experiences had been
identified and trained. And the positive responses these panelists received from
the largely non-Nikkei audiences would embolden others.

MARCH–JULY 1971: THE CONFIRMATION OF THEORIES

After heated debates over noise and other environmental concerns, Congress, on March 21, 1971, canceled the SST program. It was a devastating blow both to Boeing and to the Puget Sound region. More than 3,000 Boeing engineers were eventually terminated or transferred to other programs; the day after the cancellation, according to Henry Miyatake, about half were given pink slips. Miyatake survived a first cut and was reassigned to a temporary program. Mike Nakata went to work for General Dynamics in Quincy, Massachusetts, although he returned to Boeing a year later, in 1972.

Miyatake's temporary assignment was to a contract-termination group, which worked out how to fulfill contractual agreements with the government. When that assignment ended, in July, Miyatake met with John Hayes (not his real name), a personnel manager from Boeing's fabrication division, for a possible reassignment.

As Miyatake later recalled, Hayes said, "Looking over your record, I see all your references, all your relatives, are in Seattle. Educated here, too. Yeah, I know you people. You're not going anywhere. You have to stay here. Only place you can work. Boeing."

Miyatake was surprised by Hayes's comments. As Hayes continued talking, Miyatake realized that this man knew a lot about Japanese Americans, especially about the World War II expulsion experience. Even then, however, Miyatake did not expect what followed. Hayes pulled a document out of his files and began to read aloud:

> I am proud that I am an American citizen of Japanese ancestry, for my very background makes me appreciate more fully the wonderful advantages of this nation. I believe in her institutions, ideals, and traditions; I glory in her heritage; I boast of her history; I trust in her future. . . .
>
> Although some individuals may discriminate against me, I shall never become bitter or lose faith, for I know that such persons are not representative of the majority of the American people. . . .
>
> Because I believe in America . . . I pledge myself to . . . assume actively my duties and obligations as a citizen, cheerfully and without any reservations whatsoever, in the hope that I may become a better American in a greater America.

To Miyatake, the Japanese American Creed, written in 1941 by Mike Masaoka, the JACL national secretary during World War II, said the equivalent of "You can treat us like crap, but we're still going to be loyal." But Hayes's pulling it out and reading it to him was downright insulting. Miyatake figured that Hayes carried it around to read to all the Nisei engineers who were being demoted or released.

"Okay, here's what I've got for you," Hayes continued. "You can work in my division, but with a 25 percent pay cut."

As Miyatake later recalled this meeting, "Hayes felt that it would have taken a cataclysmic catastrophe for me to leave. Well, I had a job offer from San Francisco, and I could have left, but my children elected to stay here because of their friends and schooling and all this kind of stuff, so I just grinned and beared it."

Miyatake took the pay cut, but the meeting only reinforced his conviction that something had to be done about the perceptions of Nikkei in the United States. Headstrong as ever, Miyatake pushed ahead in his research on redress.

JAPANESE COMMUNITY CENTER PROJECT

In 1971, during the period of the massive Boeing layoffs, Chuck Kato, a Nisei civil engineer, was working with the Economic Development Administration (EDA), a federal agency that distributed funds for public works projects in areas of high unemployment. With Seattle and all of Washington State suffering so severely from Boeing's ailing health, federal funds were pumped into communities to keep the local economies going.

Because Kato knew these funds were available, and because there had been a lack of decent facilities for his kids' cultural education, he decided to organize support for a Japanese cultural center. By 1973, Kato was no longer working for the EDA, but he still knew a few people working there, as well as the types of projects that were being funded. With EDA funds going not only to schools and nonprofit organizations but also to dog pounds "and other ridiculous structures," he decided to propose his idea of a cultural center to the Japanese Language School Board, of which he had just become a member. With the rest of the board agreeing that the center was a good idea, Kato and a few others, including Boeing electrical engineer Ken Nakano, began to organize support in churches and community groups.

Nakano, a Kibei (American-born, educated in Japan), had moved from Portland to Japan at the age of six. At the time of the atomic bomb blast, he was thirteen years old and living in Hiroshima, "two kilometers from dead center." He returned to the United States after enlisting in the American forces in Japan.[21] Nakano, fluent in Japanese, was an important link to the Issei community and to the Japanese Language School Board.

Miyatake and Chuck Kato knew each other mostly because their sons were classmates at the Seattle judo dojo. Kato quickly enlisted Miyatake in the cultural center project because their sons would be direct beneficiaries of the center and because, as Kato said, "Henry was one of the smartest people I ever ran into. He knew everything about everything. He had the facts and figures, or could figure them out." Since Miyatake had already been researching the losses that Japanese Americans had suffered during their World War II expulsion and incarceration, he was able to provide data for the EDA grant proposal, explaining the losses and the effects of the expulsion, as well as the need for the Nikkei to rebuild their community.

Unfortunately, the project was never to be. Kato, while trying to organize support for the Japanese cultural center, had given out copies of his proposal to community groups and churches. "The Japanese Buddhist Church looked at our proposal and submitted one of their own," he said. "So we had two similar proposals from two different community groups. They [the EDA officials] told us, 'Get your act together,' and neither group got a cent."[22]

But the research, proposal writing, and community organizing were not a total loss. The Japanese cultural center project had brought the three engineers together. Each had learned how his respective skills could complement those of the others in community-building efforts. This mesh of talents would not go to waste.

2 / Roadblocks

He was quite enthusiastic about doing something about getting some
money from the government for our imprisonment. And I was glad to
see Henry [Miyatake] doing that. That someone was doing it. Because
I know the kind of work that involved. . . . I figured somebody has got
to start it. . . . Henry had the drive; he had the determination.

—Shosuke Sasaki[1]

Henry, Chuck [Kato], the whole group, they treat me as one of them.
And they use my talents. I feel very comfortable working with them.
I think [redress] is a very interesting project. I didn't know about [the
concentrations camps] until Henry told me. The Nisei, they're not
proud [about surviving incarceration] and [didn't] say, "I went to camp"
like they do today. In those days they don't want to talk. So I told Henry,
"You're right," so I started reading books. I read every day, so that by
the time the redress was going on, I know quite a bit. When I suggest
some things, they say, "Good job." [I felt like], "Hey, I sold my idea."
It's nice, you feel good, especially when you work at Boeing where you
seldom ever sell your idea.

—Ken Nakano[2]

SUMMER 1973: SERENDIPITY

Ben Nakagawa, president of the Seattle Chapter JACL in 1973, unable to attend
a summer board meeting, asked a vice president, Cherry Kinoshita, to conduct the session. One item on the agenda caught her eye: a memo from Barry
Matsumoto, JACL's Washington, D.C., representative. It reminded chapters
that a resolution passed at the 1970 JACL national convention supported

requesting reparations from the government. It asked what the chapters wished to do about it.

At the meeting, Kinoshita presented the request from Matsumoto and asked, without much hope that anyone would reply, if anyone wanted to volunteer to study the issue.

"I was so surprised that someone actually volunteered," Kinoshita would later say. "It was Henry."

It was a most serendipitous meeting. As Miyatake recalled,

> I wasn't involved with the JACL at that point. But we [the Asian Engineers and Technical Employees Association] were contemplating legal action against Boeing because they had put all Nikkei into a low salary category. Guys like Ken [Nakano] were working with a wiring group, pitifully treated by the Boeing Company. . . . When I had expressed this to Tomio [Moriguchi], he said, "Why don't you tell the JACL? They might be able to do something for you." And this is why I joined JACL. I had been at this meeting by coincidence . . . when Cherry asked for volunteers for reparations, well, I had done all the homework, so I thought, "Okay, let's see what I can do with it."

Miyatake turned to Mike Nakata for help.

"You gotta work with me on redress," he said. "The Boeing stuff is okay, but this is more important."

"Well, I'll get you all the help you need," Nakata responded. "But you gotta come up with a good plan."[3]

By the latter part of 1973, Miyatake had pulled his ideas together into a full presentation, "complete with flip charts." He asked Ben Nakagawa for a little time at one of the meetings to make his presentation and was promised he could speak after all other business had been taken care of.

As the November meeting dragged on, Miyatake sat and fidgeted. It was getting late, and Nakagawa had to leave. Nakagawa decided to close the meeting, but he added, "Anybody interested in hearing Henry's presentation on reparations can stay after the regular meeting." Chuck Kato, Ken Nakano, Mike Nakata, and Min Masuda all stayed to hear Miyatake's presentation. Someone Miyatake had never met before also stayed: Shosuke Sasaki, a retired statistician who had spent twenty years at Standard & Poor's in New York and had worked as a financial analyst in Denver, Colorado.

Just as Miyatake's attendance at the summer meeting had been by chance, it was fortuitous that Sasaki turned up at the November meeting. He had come at the request of Nakata, his longtime friend. Sasaki was just what this soon-to-be committee needed—someone who could write and edit. Although he had been hired at Standard & Poor's as a statistician, Sasaki had spent the latter part of his time there as a "rewrite [financial] analyst." "In fact," he said, "I was an editor of that service, although I was never paid for it." Like the Japanese American engineers at Boeing, he had seen promotions and raises pass him by. But, unlike the groups of Asian engineers at Boeing who were considering legal action against their employer, Sasaki did not worry about promotions and raises because he had been "able to get by," doing well for himself on the stock market. Notably, what Sasaki had done at Standard & Poor's was to persuade the entire American Newspaper Guild (ANG), in 1952, to stop using the term *Jap*. The guild had a policy against the "use of deroga-tory epithets in publications," and Sasaki, a member, used that policy in his successful campaign, first in the New York chapter of the ANG and then in the national organization, to add *Jap* to the guild's epithet list.[4]

As far as Nakata was concerned, Sasaki, who had retired from his job in Denver and returned to Seattle, was "God's gift" to the group of engineers.

"We needed a full-time person if we were going to go for redress," Nakata said, "and then Shosuke showed up. . . . I told Shosuke that we were going to make him famous."[5]

Sasaki does not remember Nakata's comment. About his participation, he simply said, "I've long looked at [redress] as being essentially Henry's idea, and that I was really trying to help him. . . . I was [just] the only one available . . . who had any writing experience."[6]

Miyatake had come to the JACL meeting thoroughly prepared. He had a flip chart, with sections covering the background and history of the losses suffered by Japanese Americans during World War II, the philosophy and rationale of redress, the government's policies of suppressing the culture and ethnic identity of Japanese Americans, and the destruction of economic, fam-ily, and community life. Miyatake also included a plan to win redress. This plan, later refined by Sasaki and Kato, became the basis for all redress action and education.

Miyatake was asking for $5,000 for each individual affected by the gov-ernment's actions during World War II, whether that meant Executive Order 9066, Public Law 503, or any other action that had forced people to move out of a designated area.[7] These individuals included Aleuts, Germans, Italians,

Latin American Japanese, Japanese immigrants, and Japanese Americans. On top of the base amount, Miyatake had figured in an additional $10 per day for every day spent under incarceration, again covering everyone.

The $5,000 was derived from the sum that the federal government had at that time been giving to people forced into relocation because of any federal action, such as construction of a dam; later, when the government raised its relocation allocation to $10,000, Miyatake and others would also increase their proposed amounts. The $10 per day came from the amount that the U.S. government, in 1970, had paid its armed services personnel who were prisoners of war.

These reparations, Miyatake explained, were to be paid for by a tax-checkoff plan for Japanese Americans. As Americans of Japanese ancestry paid their taxes, they would pay into the fund, and the eldest members who qualified for redress would be paid first. The tax checkoff would continue until all those who qualified for redress had been paid.[8]

The plan was unique, simple, and beautiful in conception—"a genius of an idea," as Nakata put it,[9] explaining later that it would appear to Congress as if those who had been interned were paying themselves. Other advantages were explained to another redress activist[10] in 1979: a tax-checkoff plan would avoid the "risk and uncertainty" of an annual appropriations battle. Moreover, Miyatake and Tom Koizumi, a Democratic precinct committeeman, had run projections, based on income statistics from the census, of Japanese American salaries and earning power, and they found that the estimated $7.2 billion in reparations could be paid off in seven years.

Persuasive though Miyatake's plan was for Nakata, Nakano, Kato, and Sasaki, it did not fare as well with Ben Nakagawa, who tabled the plan at the December meeting of the Seattle Chapter JACL. Nakagawa thought the funds should be used to educate the public. He also felt that Miyatake's funding plan would defeat the purpose of redress—that "if we paid ourselves, how would the society that put us [in concentration camps] ever know they were guilty of an unconstitutional injustice against us and, then, where would the closure be?"[11]

After considering Nakagawa's idea of using the funds to educate the public, Miyatake decided that an education fund was a good idea and later included it with the individual payments. "All the unclaimed money would be set aside into another fund to be used for educational purposes, scholarships, educational funds, educational research, that kind of stuff," he recalled.

However, Miyatake and the others, who later called themselves the Seattle

Evacuation Redress Committee (SERC), would quickly discover that forging political support for the plan through the community and the JACL was neither simple nor beautiful. A rocky road lay ahead.

During the summer of 1974, the JACL National Council, convening in Portland, made redress a top priority, by and large adopting the resolution of the Pacific Northwest District Council (PNWDC): the national JACL should secure an acknowledgment from the government that a gross injustice against Japanese Americans had been committed during World War II.[12] But the Seattle chapter was growing somewhat anxious and impatient over the national JACL's apparent inaction. After all, the chapter reasoned, redress had first been brought up at the 1970 convention; it had been made a JACL priority in 1972, and now, in 1974, it was again being made a priority.[13]

At its September 29, 1974, meeting, the PNWDC considered the question of reparations. Rep. George Danielson of California had introduced a bill, H.R. 15717, that provided assistance for persons affected by E.O. 9066. Money for assistance would come from a trust fund set up by the treaty allowing for the return of Okinawa to Japan. The bill was, at the time, in a subcommittee of the House Judiciary Committee. The JACL national staff was asking for the PNWDC's reaction.

During the discussion, it was brought out that the PNWDC had already supported the idea of reparations,[14] and that plans being considered by the national JACL board might conflict with Danielson's plan. Also, Ben Nakagawa and Min Masuda, both of the Seattle Chapter, "expressed opinions that the bill [made] provisions quite different from the reparations we had had in mind."[15] There was also a feeling that what was now being called for was a more detailed plan for redress. Columbia Basin Chapter president Ed Yamamoto moved to reject the Danielson Bill. Nakagawa seconded, and the motion carried. Instead, the PNWDC unanimously passed a resolution asking Tsujimura to convey to the JACL national board the urgency of taking action on the reparations resolution. The resolution also urged the national board to form a committee to recommend specific implementation of the resolution and to consider pertinent legislation and redress proposals.[16]

Deciding that the national JACL needed some help in studying redress options, the Seattle Chapter offered to pay the way for Henry Miyatake to attend a national executive board meeting and speak on redress. Sam Shoji, Seattle Chapter president at the time, wrote, in a letter dated October 17, 1974, to national president Shig Sugiyama, citing the PNWDC resolution as a basis for this unusual request:

> During the past two bienniums the issue of reparation was deemed to be one of the top priority matters of the JACL, but to date there have been no procedures or committee set up at the national level to give guidance.
>
> At the Pacific Northwest District Council meeting held in Seattle on September 28th and 29th, the District Governor, Dr. Jim Tsujimura, was given specific directions to have the matter placed on the agenda at the next National Executive Board Meeting to be held in November.
>
> In order that the National Executive Board of JACL be better informed and aware of many details involved in any type of reparation, the Seattle Chapter has asked Mr. Henry Miyatake to attend the meeting of the National Executive Board, which we understand will be on November 7, 1974. Mr. Miyatake has spent much time, energy and effort to research this matter and has a wealth of pertinent facts and information on reparations. His efforts have been . . . personal . . . because of the lack of a national movement, but he has been in contact with other individuals who have also expressed their interests.
>
> I am writing to make a specific request that Mr. Miyatake be given adequate time to make a presentation at the meeting of the National Executive Committee.

Miyatake was assigned an hour and a half on the agenda. Tomio Moriguchi, who had just been elected national treasurer, arranged for him to make his presentation at the November 7, 1974, meeting in San Francisco. Miyatake had planned for his full time allowance, including a quarter of an hour for questions. Upon his arrival at the meeting, President Sugiyama informed Miyatake, "We've got to cut your part to half an hour, and we have to fit you in at the end of the program." Miyatake felt shortchanged:

> We made the presentation. It was like talking to a bunch of disinterested people. Nobody gave a hoot. The only one who provided any kind of support was, of course, Tomio. Tomio supported it, and [Jim] Tsujimura supported it. Only one national board member, Helen Kawagoe, spoke in favor of reparations. The others were afraid that it was going to be an organizational embarrassment.

The executive board decided that this was such a heavy issue, they couldn't act on it. They decided that instead of facing the issue head on, they would create a legislative—political—action committee that would generate plans and procedures.

Worse still, as Miyatake tells it, Sugiyama and JACL national director David Ushio told him flatly, "You know, we're not in favor of what you're doing."

Disgusted and disheartened, but ever hopeful, Miyatake took his chance to push for another issue. During his legal research, he had found no mention that Executive Order 9066 had ever been rescinded. Seeing an educational opportunity, SERC had already started talking about organizing the community around the rescission of E.O. 9066. The plan was still in its infancy, but Miyatake decided to go for it anyway. "How about giving some support on trying to revoke E.O. 9066?" he asked the national leadership. The answer: "We're not interested."

Miyatake returned to Seattle irritated. He was surprised by the reaction he was getting. The people from whom he had expected the most help seemed to be thwarting his efforts.

Still, he pressed on. The Seattle Evacuation Redress Committee was sure that the support of a national organization was necessary for the bill's passage. Miyatake's research and his legal advisers had convinced him that legislative rather than judicial redress was the more fruitful path to take. If that was the case, then a large-scale movement was necessary: only a national group could mount a successful legislative campaign.

SERC began with the Pacific Northwest District Council. Jim Tsujimura invited Miyatake and SERC to present their plan at the February 2, 1975, meeting of the PNWDC. Miyatake and Koizumi found a receptive audience:

> Henry Miyatake presented a series of charts which he and Tom Koizumi had prepared on reparations, including an analysis of compensation categories, historical background of those incarcerated, bases of compensation, and a flow chart on possible funding.
>
> Henry feels that the route of legal cases offers no hope for the solution of reparation problems.
>
> The material presented is available to JACL chapters, and Henry and Tom are ready to present the program if arrangements are made. . . .

Ed Yamamoto moved that PNWDC form a reparations committee. Emi Somekawa seconded, and the motion was passed.

Governor Tsujimura commended Henry for the presentation and recommended that the committee submit a budget request. He asked each chapter president to appoint a member for the new committee and to send the name of the appointee to Henry.[17]

The Seattle Evacuation Redress Committee began to meet with local community groups, both Nikkei and non-Nikkei. The major educational tool was the flip chart, which was based on Miyatake's presentation at the Seattle Chapter JACL and PNWDC meetings, and which Chuck Kato and Shosuke Sasaki had modified. Miyatake, Kato, and Ken Nakano had discovered that the Nikkei community was not cohesive. Many were fearful of a backlash from white Americans; some just thought redress was a bad idea. But once they had listened to the entire presentation, people started to come around. There was still some resistance, but SERC's message was now being heard.

Miyatake was particularly impressed with the support his proposal received from the Japanese Baptist Church. "Reverend [Paul] Nagano recognized the moral issue, that the internment was wrong. His support was very important." Because of the response from the Baptist Church, SERC decided to address all churches that had predominantly Japanese American congregations, as well as the Nikkeijinkai and Kenjinkai, two important local Japanese community organizations.

Most were supportive, but not all the presentations went smoothly. According to Miyatake, the Seattle Buddhist Church (Seattle Betsuin) board was one church group that was not open to the idea of redress. "We had a discussion with the adult group, and they were supportive of redress, but not the board."[18]

Often at these presentations, Kato noted, the more vocal ones would express "all sorts of negative attitudes, but the ones who supported us would come up after the meeting and declare their support." Nakano, fluent in Japanese, was making presentations to the Issei. He found that most of them were for redress. It was in these sessions with the Issei that SERC found the urgency of their cause. The Issei's advancing age and ailing health were not lost on SERC. It was vital that redress be attained as soon as possible. SERC would go on to challenge every strategic proposal by the national JACL and the Nikkei politicians that it regarded as delaying and "diversionary."

In all their presentations, Miyatake was surprised to find that the "average Caucasian groups were not only supportive once they learned what had happened, they wondered what had taken us so long to do something about it." Everyone from his children's high school classmates to the United Methodists and Unitarians in Bellevue "said they'd be willing to support a congressional bill of this nature. And the *hakujin* kids, their response was, 'Why is it that it takes you twenty-five or thirty years to get off your duff?'"

These responses, and the responses to the *Pride and Shame* exhibit and panels, suggested to the Seattle Evacuation Redress Committee that the feared white backlash was minimal. Therefore, the refusal to speak out in favor of redress on the part of community organization leaders, especially those in JACL, was, to put it mildly, puzzling. As Miyatake recalled, the Caucasians supported the redress proposal. "But then we get to the Seattle [JACL] Chapter, which was kind of reticent. We get to the next level, which is more reticent. The higher you go in our Japanese American hierarchy, the worse it becomes. And here it is, a civil rights issue. They're supposed to be the organization that supports civil rights!"

Part of the reason for the national JACL's response was that few in leadership positions believed that redress had any chance of passing, and if there wasn't a chance of passage, why waste time with a campaign that could bring up the anti-Japanese attitude again? Miyatake was impatient with this "let sleeping dogs lie" posture.

Relations between the Seattle Evacuation Redress Committee and the national JACL grew worse. For Miyatake, the earlier slight during the executive board meeting foreshadowed an eye-opening lesson in JACL politics. It took place at an April 19–20, 1975, meeting of the newly formed JACL Political Education Committee (PEC), to which the national board had appointed Miyatake.

To this day, Miyatake is convinced that the meeting was a diversionary tactic. He had been given an hour and a half on the agenda of the first morning of the two-day meeting to discuss proposals for redress. His time never came. The committee's interim chair, Kaz Oshiki, an aide to Rep. Robert Kastenmeier of Wisconsin, started to talk about why it was going to be nearly impossible to pass redress legislation. Oshiki's reasoning was simple: "We got representation from California, Washington, and Oregon, and very little elsewhere in the country. We can't possibly pass a bill of any magnitude." According to Miyatake, Oshiki went on for two hours in this manner. Oshiki was followed by Min Yasui, noted defendant in one of the original test cases challenging the eviction and curfew laws, who recounted the exploits of JACL in getting Title II of the Internal Security Act repealed. As Yasui rambled on for two hours, all Miyatake could think was "This is supposed to be my time." Finally, at around noon, Oshiki told him they would have to delay his presentation until the following day. Miyatake was upset, but Oshiki simply said, "We can't help it. There's too many things on the agenda."

National JACL meetings are scheduled so that people can arrive late Friday night (or early Saturday morning) and leave by early afternoon Sunday. Meetings are scheduled to end at noon, but, because of travel considerations, many if not most people are gone by 11:30 A.M. Miyatake could see another slight coming.

As he tells it, Oshiki informed him on Sunday morning that he was scheduled for 11:30: "That means you've got only 30 minutes." Miyatake protested, explaining that his presentation was quite detailed and that he would not be able to give it in such a short time.

"No, that's what you gotta do—30 minutes," Oshiki replied.

By the time Miyatake's turn came, it was already past noon, and Oshiki informed him that he had only 10 minutes. Miyatake gave a short presentation but was cut off. His carefully prepared handouts were left on the table as everyone left.

Oshiki, questioned years later about the meeting, gave this response:

> I cannot believe that . . . I could condone that kind of arbitrary and unfair treatment of any person, . . . especially if that person were promised an hour and a half on the morning of the session. If Min Yasui and I controlled the morning session, what happened in the afternoon? Why would Henry's time be pushed back to the second morning, and until 11:30 A.M., if adjournment was set for 12 noon? . . . That would have been so grossly unfair it seems to me that, one, I couldn't have been that nasty and domineering and, two, the majority of the committee would have overruled the chair.[19]

However, Oshiki did admit that much of the meeting was spent in discussion of forming a separate nonprofit lobbying body for political purposes.

Despite these differing accounts of the meeting's details, the fact remains that the national JACL leaders showed very little interest in actually discussing reparations. Oshiki admitted as much in a memo to the PEC, in which he wrote of the meeting held April 19–20, 1975:

The initial PEC meeting did not face the reparations issue directly; rather, it suggested that committee members investigate interest in the [redress] proposal among their constituency. I am confident that, with a few exceptions, there was no burning support for it—although probably more than for any other issue. In the Pacific Southwest and in the Seattle area, we have two militant groups which are working without any visible support from national JACL.[20]

1975: THE "APPEAL FOR ACTION"

Miyatake felt insulted, and this feeling was shared by SERC and the Seattle Chapter JACL. Hearing the news of what had occurred at the meetings of the JACL national board and the Political Education Committee, the Seattle Chapter even considered completely dropping out of JACL. But SERC, still convinced that it needed the support of the national organization, decided to take redress to the grassroots level, straight to the 102 JACL chapters and chapter presidents.

SERC produced an information packet containing a powerfully pointed message, in writing and on audiotape ("An Appeal for Action to Obtain Redress for the World War II Evacuation and Imprisonment of Japanese Americans"), written by Sasaki with the aid of Miyatake and Nakata. The tape, SERC reasoned, could be played at chapter meetings. In the message, SERC charged that the "uprooting and imprisonment of Japanese Americans" was a "monstrous violation of the most basic of American traditions and laws relating to human freedom," a violation that had crowned "four decades of anti-Japanese propaganda of the most vile, outrageous and pervasive sort, particularly in the newspapers printed in the Pacific Coast states":

This propaganda brain-washed the mass of white Americans into feeling that the Japanese were subhuman creatures deserving of no rights whatever and brainwashed the Japanese Americans into thinking that they had been born of an unworthy race and that they had to submit meekly to practically any governmental trampling of their human rights in order to "prove" to others that the Nisei were "loyal Americans." The fact that even after a lapse of thirty years no real attempt has been made by Japanese Americans to obtain redress for the wrongs, humiliations and loss of income suffered by them during their totally unwarranted imprisonment indicates that the older Nisei at least, have been so psychologically crippled by their pre-war and wartime experience that they have been unable to act as Americans should.

Passive submission or self-abasement when confronted by government tyranny or injustice was alien to the beliefs held by the founders of this nation. If, in the face of British government tyranny, they had acted like the Nisei have in the face of American government tyranny, there would be no 200th Anniversary of the founding of our country to celebrate. In commemorating the birth of our nation, therefore, it is time that Americans of Japanese ancestry repudiate the pseudo-American doctrine, promoted by white racists and apparently believed in by some former Nisei leaders, that there is one kind of Americanism for whites and another kind for non-whites. If Japanese Americans are as American as the J.A.C.L. has often claimed, then they should act like Americans and make every effort to seek redress through legislation and the courts for the rape of almost all their "unalienable rights" by the United States Government over thirty years ago.[21]

To redress the wrongs, humiliations, and loss of income, the message asked that a flat $5,000 be awarded to all who had been evacuated, plus $10 a day for each day of incarceration. To be sure that there was some legal basis for the claims made in the message, a copy was sent to Charles Z. Smith, then an associate dean at the University of Washington Law School. Smith concluded that the message calling for action was "exceptionally well done."[22]

SERC's contacts, taken together, extended to a large network of local Nikkei. Many members of the redress committee had also been part of the fundraising team for Seattle Keiro, a nursing home that was being established for Nikkei elders. SERC went back to the same groups from which its members had earlier collected money for Seattle Keiro. Now they discussed redress and the "Appeal for Action." Some of these groups, like the Japanese Baptist, Blaine Methodist, and St. Peter's Episcopal congregations and the Nikkeijinkai, contributed money for reproduction of the tapes.

Chuck Kato and Henry Miyatake remember most vividly the meeting with the Nisei Veterans Committee (NVC, or Nisei Vets). According to Mitatake, it turned into a shouting match: "It was worse than the VFW [Veterans of Foreign Wars]. The VFW accused us, 'You guys bombed Pearl Harbor!' That's just ignorance. Some of the Nisei Vets shouted at us, calling us, 'Traitors!' Then Chuck got really mad. He started shouting back, using words I never heard him use before."

Because Kato, Ken Nakano, and Miyatake were all veterans, too, they were particularly upset when one of the Nisei Vets said, "Everything we fought for, you guys are destroying!"

"Listen," Miyatake countered, "what you guys fought for is our perfect right, the *constitutional* right." The three must have been somewhat convincing: according to Miyatake and Kato, the NVC contributed $100 for the tapes.

By November 1975 enough money had been raised to produce and mail 200 copies of audiotapes, transcripts, and a questionnaire that was to be filled out by members after listening to the tape at one of their chapter meetings. Packets were mailed to JACL chapter presidents across the country and to the national board as well as to Sens. Daniel Inouye and Spark Matsunaga of Hawaii, the entire congressional delegations of Washington and Oregon, Rep. Norman Mineta of California, and selected other California representatives. Nikkei newspapers and Nikkeijinkai (Japanese community organizations) across the country received the "Appeal for Action," as did members of the larger Nikkei community.[23] Of the 102 chapters to which packets were sent, 44 responded by April 1976.

With its questionnaire, SERC was essentially trying to find out the same thing that Barry Matsumoto had tried to find out two years earlier: What was the general consensus of the chapters with regard to redress? And, unlike Matsumoto, SERC did receive some response, but Miyatake was again disappointed: he had wanted everyone to respond. "They had a stamped envelope, everything. All they had to do was put in the contents of the survey, mark it up, sign the guy's name, put it in the envelope, and send it," he would later say.

But SERC hadn't considered the nature of many of the JACL chapters, which saw themselves primarily as social organizations and held perhaps two meetings a year, which were really parties or potluck gatherings. Given the context, a 40 percent response rate was remarkable. In addition, most of the Nikkei papers had printed the entire text of the "Appeal for Action," and all of these papers had included individual response forms for the survey questions. A summary of these responses was published in late 1975 and early 1976, showing that 85 to 95 percent of the respondents were in favor of redress. Miyatake's disappointment notwithstanding, 778 board and regular-chapter JACL members had responded by April 26, 1976.

The results were encouraging. After listening to the taped message that had been sent to them, almost all the recipients were in full or partial agreement with the appeal; only 2.7 percent were opposed. The answers to partic-ular questions spoke for themselves:[24]

Funding
Direct congressional appropriations 30.5%
Bootstrap method (tax checkoff) 69.5%

Disbursement
Individual payments 89.0%
Block grants to organizations 11.0%

Issei Priority
In favor 96.7%
Against 3.3%

Opinion of Proposed Payment Amount
($5,000 and $10 per day)
Amount is reasonable 76.6%
Amount is excessive 0.9%
Amount is grossly inadequate 28.5%

Willingness to Support Reparations
Legislation
Unwilling 5.6%
Willing 94.4%

Just as the Nikkei community's involvement with the *Pride and Shame* exhibit had demonstrated a few years earlier, the community was beginning to wake up from its reluctance to discuss its evacuation and imprisonment. Unlike the national JACL leaders, many Japanese Americans across the coun-try were now beginning to agree that those who had been wronged should have the wrongs redressed.

S. I. HAYAKAWA

The "Appeal for Action" also caught the attention of S. I. Hayakawa, an edu-cator and semanticist who had gained national prominence by taking a firm stand against dissident students while serving as president of San Francisco State University during the late 1960s and early 1970s. In a syndicated col-umn published on February 3, 1976, in the *Seattle Times,* Hayakawa attacked the "Appeal for Action" and, showing careless disregard for facts, called the members of the Seattle Chapter JACL "third-generation Japanese Americans eagerly conforming to the radical-chic fads of their non-Japanese college contemporaries." To the appeal's charge that the expulsion and incarceration were the result of the government's racist policies, Hayakawa wrote, "They [Seattle Chapter JACL members] ignore the fact that a war was going on and that, during those first awful months, the Allies were losing the war in the Pacific, so that a Japanese attack on or invasion of the West Coast was by no means unthinkable:

> The fact that Americans did not panic at the presence of Japanese immigrants in their midst, the fact that angry mobs did not descend on Japanese communities, shooting and looting and burning homes (as they had done earlier in history against the Chinese), shows that by 1941 American racial attitudes, even with the war going on, had matured profoundly since the end of the 19th century.[25]

In an op-ed piece that appeared in the *Seattle Times* the following week, Sasaki fired off a response on behalf of SERC:

> In Hayakawa's claim that a possibility of an invasion of the Pacific Coast states by the Japanese Army justified the wholesale exile of Japanese Americans, it is significant that he remains silent about the situation in Hawaii. There the Japanese Americans were not subjected to mass uprooting and imprisonment despite the fact that Hawaii was far more likely to be the place for a landing by the Japanese armed forces, before any similar landing could be attempted on the Pacific Coast.
>
> Hayakawa also apparently feels that because the Japanese Americans were not subjected to wholesale looting, murder and arson by mobs in 1942, it is highly improper for Japanese Americans to seek redress over their mere evacuation and imprisonment. This is akin to saying that a woman who has been raped should not demand justice against her violator, because the man had refrained from robbing or murdering her.
>
> In his disordered disaffection for the Seattle JACL and the younger generation, he has taken some shots at the Sansei (third-generation Japanese Americans) which were both wildly misdirected and totally unjustified.
>
> First, that "Appeal for Action" was written by a 63-year-old Issei (a retired financial analyst), with the aid and collaboration of a Nisei welding engineer who is 58 years old and a Nisei system engineer who is 46 years old.

All three retain vivid memories of the evacuation and imprisonment they suffered during World War II.

Second, over two-thirds of the membership of the Seattle JACL is composed of Issei and Nisei. On the whole, its Sansei members are a well-educated, serious, and responsible group. For Hayakawa to describe them as "radical-chic" is a gross insult.[26]

This was not the last time that the Seattle JACL and the larger Nikkei community would face off against Hayakawa. In November 1976 Hayakawa was elected to the U.S. Senate from California, becoming the first Japanese American senator from the continental United States. Sen. Hayakawa would become one of the most outspoken foes of the national redress movement.

1976: RESCISSION, STOLEN CREDIT, AND A PEN

An honest reckoning . . . must include a recognition of our national mistakes as well as our national achievements. Learning from our mistakes is not pleasant, but as a great philosopher once admonished, we must do so if we want to avoid repeating them.

—President Gerald R. Ford

Because Miyatake had not seen any reference to rescission of Executive Order 9066 during his research at the University of Washington Law School library (see chapter 1), SERC was still considering some action around the issue. Despite the national JACL's lack of enthusiasm, Miyatake researched the issue further and met with legal scholars and concluded that the order had never been officially revoked after World War II. Seeing a great opportunity for public education, he decided that a presidential revocation was in order.

A position paper on rescission was drafted by SERC after strategy meetings in July and August 1975, with Sasaki, Tomio Moriguchi, Mike Nakata, Ken Nakano, and Tom Koizumi in attendance. Koizumi and Miyatake decided that the quickest line to the White House was through Washington's governor, Dan Evans, who was a friend of Vice President Nelson Rockefeller and had been high on President Ford's list of possible vice presidents before Rockefeller was named.

Miyatake felt that Koizumi, being "into the political scene" through his involvement with Democratic precinct committees, would be the best person to negotiate something with Evans. "I'm not very good at being diplomatic," was Miyatake's comment.

Koizumi and Miyatake decided to contact Koizumi's friend Ruth Yoneyama Woo, who had worked as a receptionist in the governor's office until 1972, and who still had contacts with Evans's staff. Woo and Phil Hayasaka, former director of the Seattle Human Rights Commission, set up a meeting at Seattle Center with Miyatake, Koizumi, Nakano, and Evans's chief of staff, James Dolliver.

According to Miyatake, Dolliver doubted the findings of their research. He was astounded to hear that E.O. 9066 was still in place, and he told them he would look into the matter and get back to them. A week and a half later, he called Miyatake.

"I guess you're right," he said. "What are you going to do about it?"

"What can we do?"

"Well," said Dolliver, "I'll go further, and I'll ask the governor if he wants me to take some action."

Dolliver then arranged a meeting with Evans and the group. At that meeting, Evans pledged his personal support for the rescission effort.

According to Paul Isaki, writing in the *Hokubei Mainichi,* a bilingual community paper in San Francisco,

> At Governor Evans' direction, James Dolliver made at least two trips to Washington D.C. in September, 1975, to discuss the Seattle JACL's revocation proposal with various members of the White House staff. On those occasions he met with Gwen Anderson, Dudley Chapman and others on President Ford's staff, as well as Dick Allison of the Vice President's staff. It is important to note that Governor Evans is held in very high regard by the President, and the weight of the governor's support for the proposal was largely responsible for the revocation proposal being considered and ultimately approved by the White House. In any event, it was decided that a Presidential revocation of E.O. 9066 could be accomplished, and the necessary steps were initiated within the White House to draft a proclamation for President Ford's signature at a ceremony scheduled for February 19, 1976—the 34th anniversary of E.O. 9066.
>
> At this point Mr. Dolliver suggested that it was appropriate for citizens of Japanese ancestry to be publicly identified as the prime movers behind the revocation effort. He therefore assigned Mich Matsudaira, executive director of the governor's Asian American Affairs Commission, to coordi-

nate final arrangements on behalf of the governor. Matsudaira was directed to work with Wayne Horiuchi, national JACL representative in Washington D.C., to secure the support of JACL chapters and members of Congress.[27]

According to Matsudaira, sometime in November 1975 Dolliver informed him, "It looks like it's going to happen. We just needed some publicity to come out. Get hold of the JACL." Matsudaira says the support from congressional leaders had already been attained: "What we wanted was a groundswell of publicity. It was necessary so that when it came out, the media was prepared. . . . The whole idea was to have a platform to jump off onto the redress thing. So it was going to be a good chance for national attention for redress."

Matsudaira contacted David Ushio, national JACL director, and national JACL representative Wayne Horiuchi. Both were excited to have this project placed in their hands. Ushio, according to Matsudaira, said this was the first he had heard of the rescission attempt, despite the fact that the PNWDC had passed the rescission appeal in September and Miyatake had raised the issue with him in 1974, at the first national board meeting he attended, right after his presentation on redress was cut off. What upset Matsudaira, however, was Ushio's attitude. They didn't need to get all the chapters involved in the rescission ceremony, Ushio told him: "We'll just call some people."

According to Matsudaira, the whole plan for national publicity was subverted by Horiuchi. In a memo sent out to national board members, Horiuchi wrote:

> A public announcement and campaign was not initiated by me for three reasons: (1) there was not enough time to mount a national campaign, (2) my White House contact advised that a public campaign was not necessary and (3) a public campaign would have encouraged every ultra right wing "nut" to write the White House and endanger the chances of rescinding the Order. (If you'll recall a poll was taken in California several years ago which showed a majority of Californians condoning the evacuation of the Japanese American during WW II).[28]

Dolliver said he would check in with Miyatake periodically to let him know how things were going. In addition, Miyatake was making calls to Gwen Anderson, his contact in the White House Domestic Affairs Office, because the wording of the rescission order was being discussed. At one point, he engaged in a heated discussion with the White House on whether to have the signing on December 7, 1975, or February 19, 1976, the 34th anniversary of E.O. 9066. December 7 was definitely out, Miyatake explained to the staff: E.O. 9066 was not to be connected with the bombing of Pearl Harbor; that was what the government had done in 1942. Miyatake reminded the staff that 1976 was also the bicentennial of the signing of the Declaration of Independence (the founding of the United States of America), and that February 19, 1976, therefore presented a better media opportunity. During this period, Miyatake discovered that he was in trouble with his superiors at Boeing: he had been working on a classified project, his phone records revealed a lot of calls to the governor's office and the White House, and Boeing officials wondered what Miyatake's work had to do with the White House Domestic Affairs Office or the governor. Since it had nothing to do with either, he was reprimanded and put on probation, with a pay cut.

According to Ushio, the Domestic Affairs Office notified the national JACL two days before the signing of the rescission order, telling JACL to be ready and handing off the task of inviting community members to the ceremony. Ushio invited only his supporters. As he said later to Bill Hosokawa, "Those people were there because they had been strong supporters of JACL and strong supporters of mine. We were in a position to make choices between people who were stabbing me in the back and people who were bending over backwards to help me."[29]

When Gov. Evans was informed that the signing would soon take place, Dolliver alerted Mich Matsudaira to be ready at any time to travel to Washington, D.C., because Matsudaira would need to represent the governor at the ceremony. Two days later, on February 18, Dolliver tracked Matsudaira down in Seattle's International District, where he was making his regular visits to community organizations. Matsudaira was told to catch a red-eye flight to Washington that night. At 9 P.M. the same evening, Henry Miyatake heard on his telephone answering machine a message telling him to get an overnight flight and be at the White House in the morning; he wasn't told what was going to happen. It was too late to arrange a flight, so Miyatake found out about the signing of the rescission order only the next morning.

At the White House, Matsudaira later said, the reception room was filled with a lot of JACLers who "were never involved" beforehand, and who had even spoken against the rescission attempt in the first place. "They all snubbed me," he recalled. "They treated me like, 'What am I doing there?'"

In setting up the signing and the photo, Gwen Anderson placed Matsudaira next to President Ford, but at the last minute Sen. Inouye was moved up front, along with Ushio and Columbia Basin Chapter president Ed Yamamoto. Matsudaira was pushed off to the side and given a consolation prize: three pens. At the reception afterward, Matsudaira recalls, when people asked him why he had the three pens, he told them that two of the pens were for the Seattle Chapter JACL and the State of Washington, which had springboarded the whole effort. "This is the acknowledgment," he said. The initial idea and much of the work had been Henry Miyatake's, but not only had he not known the signing was going to take place, he was left with little more than part of a pen.

The rescission ceremony turned out to be a great media opportunity. The televised signing was on all the national network news programs, and, for the first time, a United States president issued the words that Japanese Americans had been waiting 36 years to hear:

> We now know what we should have known then—not only was that evac-
> uation wrong, but Japanese-Americans were and are loyal Americans. On the
> battlefield and at home, Japanese-Americans—names like Hamada, Mitsu-
> mori, Marimoto, Noguchi, Yamasaki, Kido, Munemori and Miyamura—
> have been and continue to be written in our history for the sacrifices and
> the contributions they have made to the well-being and security of this, our
> common Nation.[30]

"An American Promise," as Ford's rescission statement was titled, would later be used in JACL's redress materials.

1976: THE NATIONAL JACL BACKTRACKS

At the September 1974 Pacific Northwest District Council meeting, the council requested that Jim Tsujimura, district governor, urge the national board to get moving on the issue of redress. Also at that meeting, Tsujimura said that he had been instructed to contact Mike Masaoka, the recently retired JACL representative in Washington, D.C., to convince him of the validity of redress. After frequent contacts, Masaoka assured Tsujimura that he would write an article about redress in the *Pacific Citizen*, the national publication of JACL.[31]

In the 1975 *Pacific Citizen Holiday Issue*, Masaoka laid out the historical data of the expulsion, the validity of reparations, the types of plans offered, the possible pitfalls associated with the plans, and the reasons why JACL should take an active part in securing redress. He believed that both Congress and the courts would be more sympathetic to reparations

> if whatever is determined to be the "reasonable reparations" would be placed in public trust, to be administered possibly by the JACL and to be used for certain specified purposes such as scholarships and loans to the children and grandchildren of the evacuees, special retirement and medical treatments for evacuees who require such attention possibly because of the Evacuation experience, special programs and projects to help the major Japanese American communities resolve their special problems, including cultural and meeting centers, etc.[32]

He also stated that a JACL reparations project "may provide the 'cause' around which most members and friends can rally" and could be "the beginning of an inspired national public educational and political campaign that will motivate more JACLers than any issue of recent date."

Nevertheless, Masaoka's favoring of a trust fund for dispensing funds to community groups was not what SERC had in mind for reparations. And, according to Miyatake, both Masaoka and national JACL leaders began to hedge on redress in later articles for the *Pacific Citizen*.

On May 8–9, 1976, Ed Yamamoto convened the National Reparations Campaign (REPACAMP) in Portland to consider redress proposals currently on the table and to make a recommendation to the upcoming national convention in June. One plan was SERC's, the so-called Seattle plan; the other plan was Yamamoto's, the Columbia Basin plan, which favored two trust funds, one for educational purposes and one for U.S.–Japanese cultural exchange.[33]

While REPACAMP was working out its recommendations to the National JACL Council, SERC members were working on another angle. SERC had decided that JACL's hedging on redress was the result of Masaoka's opposition. Shosuke Sasaki, who had worked with Masaoka to get the term *Jap* added to the American Newspaper Guild's epithet list, wrote to him and asked to meet with him for a discussion of his position on redress. In two days of meetings that preceded the convention, Miyatake says, he and Sasaki and Kato answered every one of Masaoka's arguments against their plan, and they received his word that he would publicly argue for redress at the upcoming convention.[34]

At the convention, after a "rousing" Masaoka statement of support, the

JACL National Council unanimously passed a motion endorsing the concept of reparations and a program for a national JACL reparations committee.[35] The motion also authorized adequate funding for the national JACL reparations committee.[36] As a result, the JACL National Reparations Committee, chaired by Edison Uno, was formed.[37]

According to Miyatake, the national convention voted for the Seattle plan in its entirety, and so he was dismayed when, immediately after the convention, Masaoka began publicly favoring a "block grant" redress payment plan, with funds to be disbursed by an organization for projects instead of being paid directly to individuals. The Seattle Chapter JACL and SERC were wary of a national Japanese American group's receiving and distributing government funds. They were certain that such a plan would mean that the Pacific Northwest and areas where few Japanese Americans resided would be shortchanged. Also, SERC reasoned, since individuals, not organizations, had experienced expulsion, internment, and loss of constitutional rights, redress was owed to individuals. Moreover, although the national Japanese American group was not specified, few in SERC doubted that the organization would be JACL or some new group dominated by JACL members. This was troublesome because many in the Japanese American community seriously mistrusted JACL's intentions. They believed that JACL at the national level was complicit in the expulsion and incarceration to begin with.[38]

National JACL Reparations Committee chair Edison Uno suffered a stroke and died during the 1976 holiday season. Mike Honda was appointed chair of the committee, which met infrequently during the first half of 1977. SERC and the PNWDC were upset by this inaction, and so Jim Tsujimura, who had been elected national JACL vice president for research and services and was in charge of redress, asked Honda to step down as chair. Honda obliged.[39]

At a reunion of Japanese Americans from the Tacoma area, Ken Nakano met Clifford Uyeda, a pediatrician from San Francisco who had led the successful national campaign to obtain a pardon for Iva Toguri.[40] Nakano explained to Uyeda that a chair was being sought for the National JACL Reparations Committee. Uyeda replied that he had not been interned. Nakano's interpretation of this statement was "He didn't refuse," and he relayed this information to Tsujimura, who called Uyeda, asking him to reconsider. Uyeda's work on the Toguri case had made him the logical person to lead a national campaign, Tsujimura said.[41] Uyeda finally agreed to take on the duties of the chair, having decided that he might be able to develop a national strategy for a redress campaign.

It was of immediate importance to Uyeda that 200 "leaders of the organization" be polled (confidentially). He felt it was a priority to know how they felt before any strategy was devised. He also felt that, by promising confidentiality, he would receive candid opinions, and he did. "I asked them, 'Are you for or against redress? And why?' . . . When the replies came in, I was shocked. The majority were not in favor of seeking redress from the federal government. I knew immediately that the re-education of the Nisei themselves was the first priority in seeking redress."[42]

The National JACL Reparations Committee then began to run a series of articles in the *Pacific Citizen*. The articles, written in consultation with committee members Ken Hayashi of Los Angeles, Peggy Nagae of Portland, and Raymond Okamura of Berkeley, were part of the committee's efforts "to clarify the issues for Japanese Americans, without whose understanding and support the project cannot go into the next phase of educating and gathering support of the American public."[43] The series was also intended to educate and inform the membership about redress and related subjects before the 1978 convention in Salt Lake City. The goal of the committee was the "development of a single realistic proposal which had wide support not only of Japanese Americans but other Americans as well," Uyeda said. "Legislative passage is the issue to which the proposal must be addressed."[44] In May, the committee reported that the task of the National JACL Reparations Committee would soon be over, and that a new committee would soon be formed, one that didn't have the word *reparations* as part of its name.[45] Also in May, the committee produced a widely distributed booklet, *The Japanese American Incarceration: A Case for Redress*.

At the national convention, in July 1978, the National JACL Reparations Committee proposed redress legislation that would award $25,000 to each individual and would set up a community trust fund. The proposal for a $25,000 individual payment had been developed by the redress representatives of each of the JACL districts, who had met in the spring of 1978. Uyeda said, "We knew of Seattle's figure of $15,000 per individual. Bill Marutani stated that the figure was too low, that by the time Congress got through with that figure it could easily be less than half that amount. 'Let's begin with $25,000,' he stated."[46]

The proposal was overwhelmingly passed by the national council, which also elected Clifford Uyeda national president, marking the first time that anyone had been elected president without first having been a chapter president or district officer.[47] Uyeda appointed John Tateishi, an instructor at City

College of San Francisco, chair of the newly formed National Committee for Redress (Tateishi had been chair of the redress committee for the San Francisco JACL chapter).

The convention, notable for having passed the proposed redress resolution and elected the redress chair to the presidency, also had as main speaker at its Sayonara Ball the newly elected senator from California, S. I. Hayakawa, who had earlier spoken out against SERC's "Appeal for Action." According to Bill Hosokawa's account of the evening, Hayakawa "launched into a lecture admonishing Japanese Americans to stop looking back and concern themselves with the problems ahead." After his statements, the media questioned the senator further, and he was then quoted as saying that the JACL had "no right" to ask for reparations, and that the notion of individual payments of $25,000 was "ridiculous."[48]

COMMISSION, ANYONE?

At an early September 1978 meeting of the National Committee for Redress, John Tateishi reported that an alternative approach to legislative action had been suggested.[49] According to the meeting minutes,

> Ron Ikejiri, JACL Washington [D.C.] Representative, has stated that [Sen. Daniel] Inouye won't sponsor our proposed legislation with a $25,000 price tag on it. He did, however, suggest that we pursue the idea of presenting a bill in Congress to establish a study commission to investigate the redress issue. . . . Ikejiri also reported that [Rep. Norman] Mineta supports this approach. The distinct advantage of the commission approach is that it would give us free publicity since Congressional hearings would be held in various parts of the country, and a Congressional committee would add credibility to the issue. . . . The distinct disadvantage is that it would take perhaps a year to constitute the commission plus an additional year before a recommendation from the commission to Congress would be submitted. Open to discussion.[50]

The ensuing discussion centered mostly on the delay engendered by such a proposal. The consensus seemed to be that the considerable amount of energy and time expended would be better directed toward an appropriations bill, perhaps to be submitted as early as 1979. But

Tateishi indicated again that Inouye didn't feel he could sponsor our bill with the $25,000 amount but was generally in favor of redress, and since the commission idea was his recommendation, we should perhaps give it some thought. . . .

Miyatake stated that perhaps [Sen. Warren] Magnuson [of Washington State] could be used to influence Inouye since Magnuson is sympathetic to our cause and was at one time Inouye's mentor in the Senate. No direction given to this idea, although it was agreed that it will be important that Nikkei Congressmen support us. Miyatake added that Magnuson could sponsor the bill and probably would be able to get it through the Ways and Means Committee by politicking. [Raymond] Okamura felt that the bill should be sponsored by a Japanese American senator, preferably Inouye since he has seniority and has more power and influence in the Senate.[51]

Miyatake's idea was dismissed, but other committee members continued to raise additional objections to the idea of a commission. Tateishi argued in favor of it, suggesting that one strategy would be to stack the hearings with informed, pro-redress people. Others answered that the hearings could not be controlled; Min Yasui and Ellen Endo, National Committee for Redress media chair and a vice president for standards and ethics at the American Broadcasting Company, cautioned that public hearings generate a lot of opposition. But the major objection was the likely delay of at least two years before the commission would submit its recommendations. Miyatake noted that Native Alaskan Land Claims Settlement Act hearings had lasted for three years.[52] Tateishi asked for a straw vote:

None were in favor of the Congressional commission idea, five were in favor of a direct appropriations bill with the possibility of submitting it early in 1979; two abstentions, Mamiya and Yasui, both of whom felt that we needed further guidance from Congressional people in Washington before making a decision: Okamura suggested that Tateishi and Mamiya go to Washington as soon as possible to confer, along with [Ron] Ikejiri and Mike Masaoka, with Japanese American Congressmen. The committee as a whole concurred with this.[53]

Tateishi did as he was instructed, sending letters to the Nikkei congressional delegation on September 26 and asking for a meeting in San Francisco with the National Committee on Redress after the current congressional session had closed.[54]

But a few days after the early September meeting, Sen. Inouye sent a letter to Uyeda, saying that he had "grave reservations about the wisdom of proposing" redress legislation. Inouye added:

> There was no doubt that former internees lost a great deal from their tragic experiences in the camps . . . to ask Congress, however, to appropriate $25,000 to each internee or his survivor, seems to me an ill-timed request. There now exists a strong sentiment among many members of Congress that the government has, perhaps, bent over too far backwards in attempting to redress the wrongs committed against native Americans. This backlash affects legislation involving American Indian affairs.
>
> And, just in the last few days, Hawaii suffered a defeat when the House rejected a proposal to create a commission to study the matter of reparations to native Hawaiians who lost their land during the unlawful overthrow of the Hawaii monarchy by the American Government.
>
> I realize that it is unfair for Japanese-Americans to be categorized with native American groups, because their problems and history differ so greatly. But from a pragmatic political standpoint, I foresee much difficulty in obtaining successful consideration of the JACL proposal at this time, due in large part to this "backlash" I have described.[55]

The meeting between the National Committee for Redress and the Nikkei congressmen was set for January 30, 1979.[56] But before it could take place, two events changed the mood, attitudes, and course of Japanese America: Seattle's election of Mike Lowry to the House of Representatives, and the Puyallup Day of Remembrance.

3 / Remembrance

For a long time I've had the disquieting feeling that, perhaps, our government wishes to minimize the evacuation event and, if this is so, there is a possibility that the evacuation event might be lost to our future generations.

We will not buy that. Therefore, it is necessary to continue to tell white America about us, as white America needs to continue to share and know us.

Because this time, we are going to walk down that long road into American history together.

—Monica Sone[1]

The JACL National Council's approval, at its summer convention, of a redress plan of $25,000 per individual had stirred great media interest. In turn, U.S. Sen. S. I. Hayakawa had begun to speak out publicly against such payments. Wanting to take advantage of some of the national attention that redress was starting to gain, the Seattle Evacuation Redress Committee contemplated some kind of "dramatic action."

Onto the scene walked Frank Chin, a tall Chinese American writer, actor, and stage director with a commanding voice and pen that resonated with fresh ideas, scathing commentary, unbounded energy, and cutting humor. Chin had also founded the Asian American Theater Workshop, in San Francisco, but he was in Seattle researching and writing a story about redress for the *Seattle Weekly*. He recognized both the attraction and the importance of the story. "I thought Japanese America had recovered its conscience and was at last making a stand for Japanese American integrity and reclaiming its history. I thought it was bold," he told Frank Abe, Seattle seaman and journalist, graduate of the University of California at Santa Cruz with a bachelor's degree in directing, and founding member of the Asian American Theater Workshop.[2]

Chin's research led him to Henry Miyatake, Shosuke Sasaki, and the rest of SERC, where "people were just waiting to do something," he said in an interview. Thus, when Chin received a call from Ene Riisna, a producer of ABC's *20/20,* asking if he had a story for a slow Thanksgiving weekend, he offered her the story of Japanese Americans in Seattle who were returning that weekend to the Puyallup Fairgrounds. A homecoming, he called it.

Riisna was sold. Chin called Miyatake and Sasaki and promised them national media attention. Then he went over to see Frank Abe, who, enjoying the off season, was contemplating painting his house.

"Abe," Chin said, "if Japanese America loses redress, you can kiss Japanese American art good-bye."[3]

That was enough to convince Abe. Chin, Abe, and Kathy Wong, another founding member of the Asian American Theater Workshop, set up camp in David Ishii's bookstore, in Pioneer Square, and attacked, with a vengeance, the organizing of this Thanksgiving weekend homecoming. They treated the Day of Remembrance (DOR), as they called it, as an elaborate play to be produced.

Miyatake had wanted the DOR to be held on February 19, 1979, but Chin thought the time to strike was immediately, before public interest died. From the time of the national JACL convention, in August, the issue had been receiving a lot of play in the media, and Chin had the *20/20* Thanksgiving weekend slot lined up; they couldn't lose the exposure. Therefore, November 25, 1978, the day after Thanksgiving, was set as the date, and the DOR steering committee—a mix of performing artists, engineers, and Sasaki, whom Chin referred to as the "conscience of the group"—began its work.[4]

Chin enlisted Abe's help on October 8, only 47 days before opening night of the DOR. This production had no script, no confirmed site, and a really iffy live audience. The members of the steering committee had only Chin's evangelical zeal and directorial skills, and SERC's experience in organizing a broad spectrum of the community, to guide them. Of course, the possibility of a nationally televised program about redress and the wartime incarceration also helped.

Although Chin scripted the plan very tightly, SERC's input—and especially Miyatake's—was vital to the event's success. Miyatake was adamant about the event being "something you could bring your family to." According to Abe,

Early on, Chin suggested a protest where we'd chain ourselves to the fence at Puyallup. First, Henry wouldn't go for it, and, secondly, it wasn't necessary, because once Henry, and Shosuke [Sasaki] and Ken [Nakano], approached the [Puyallup Western Washington Fair Association] Board, they welcomed us inside. And the whole event was planned not as a protest but as a family event, symbolized by the potluck. Frank [Chin] was always impressed by Nikkei potluck, and the idea of potluck was to defuse any political tension. The Nisei could recognize it as a family event, and for any Lillian Baker types—how can you picket a potluck? It was a very conscious, strategic decision.[5]

The potluck idea also defused a lot of the objections raised by some of the Fair Association Board. Miyatake, Sasaki, and Nakano had gone before the board to request its permission for (and cooperation in) the use of the Puyallup Fairgrounds and, perhaps, a waiver of the fee. After a heated debate, the board granted the Day of Remembrance Committee's request.

For both Sasaki and Miyatake, going to Puyallup was both auspicious and exhilarating. Chin ran into the two in Seattle's International District soon after they returned from Puyallup. As Chin wrote later,

"You know," Shosuke said, in a mood to speak in whole sentences, "I was a little leery of going out there. I haven't set foot on those premises since the days it was Camp Harmony. And, much to my surprise, all the horrible feelings and memories I expected to assail me there were of no matter. Standing there by that grandstand, alone with Henry there tonight, I found to be the strangest elation. . . ."

"I'm free! I'm free!" Henry Miyatake yelled, not too loud, and jumped up and down, and nodded at Shosuke.

"Shosuke, you didn't!" I said, and realized we looked dumb chatting and jumping in the middle of a Chinatown street.

"It wasn't until I was standing there tonight that I really felt released from camp. I think it was because I went there of my own free will."[6]

Other members of the DOR steering committee had been lining up community support, which ranged from churches to students, Issei and Nisei groups, and other Puget Sound JACL chapters. By the end of October, enough details had been worked out for an invitation to be issued:

BORN IN SEATTLE

The Memory of
One Hundred Twenty Thousand Three Hundred and Thirteen
Issei, Nisei, Sansei and others of Japanese ancestry
request the pleasure of your company for

A DAY OF REMEMBRANCE

Remember the concentration camps
stand for redress with your family
on
Saturday, November 25, 1978

join the caravan at 12 Noon—
Sick's Stadium Parking Lot Rainier Ave. S. and McClellan
and ride to what was once "Camp Harmony" and
home to 7,200 Japanese Americans.

ENTER PUYALLUP FAIRGROUNDS
at 2 pm
and
Raise the flag over Camp Harmony to remember the years of hardship
Japanese America endured to make the United States home for their parents,
themselves, their children, and all the Nikkei generations to come.

And, in smaller letters on the bottom:

Bring potluck for dinner at 6 P.M. at Camp Harmony with the people who
went to camp. If you are not able to bring potluck, please register at the
number listed below by Nov. 18th, so that adequate provisions will be provided. Come as you are. Come with your family. For your convenience, carry
the following in a satchel or tote bag: blanket, pillow or cushion, small tarp
or groundcloth.

The appealing message, on flyers, posters, press releases, and formal-
looking invitations, hit the streets and mailboxes in early November. Just a
few weeks earlier, Chin's article "How Shall Injustice Be Served?" had been
published in the *Seattle Weekly* as a refresher course on the World War II incar-

ceration, featuring profiles of Miyatake, Sasaki, and others. Op-ed pieces began appearing in the local dailies. And in the midst of all this activity, an important congressional election campaign was taking place.

At an October 1978 political fundraiser at Quong Tuck, a cozy upstairs restaurant in the International District, Henry Miyatake approached Mike Lowry, Democratic candidate for the U.S. House of Representatives from the Seventh Congressional District of Washington. Lowry's campaign scheduler, Peggy Maze, introduced the two to each other. Maze and Miyatake worked together in the Neighbors in Need food-bank program, and Miyatake had already summarized the proposed redress bill for her.

In his usual no-nonsense manner, Miyatake shook the candidate's hand and went right to the point. Believing that because Maze was already familiar with the redress proposal, Lowry might also have knowledge of it, Miyatake posed his question abruptly: "Will you support a bill for Japanese American redress?"

Lowry, a little taken aback, thought a second or two and then looked Miyatake in the eye. "Yes, of course."

Lowry later said that he was aware people were surprised by his answer, but that they should not have been, given that he had "strong feelings about this and related types of invasion of civil liberties all [his] life" and that he "was most familiar with the internment." His father and his aunt, living in eastern Washington in 1943, had seen Minidoka, the Idaho concentration camp, and his parents had always talked about "what a terribly unfair thing it was."[7]

At the time of the Quong Tuck fundraiser, Lowry, a King County Council member, was challenging the incumbent, Rep. Jack Cunningham. Miyatake had garnered Cunningham's support for a redress bill, but Cunningham had then decided that the issue was becoming a little too hot. Three months before the election, according to Miyatake, Cunningham's aide called to say that they could no longer support redress: Cunningham's polling indicated that he would lose more votes than he would gain by supporting it. Even when Miyatake talked to the candidate himself, Cunningham would not change his mind.

"I'm gonna lose too many votes," he explained.

"Well, then, you're going to lose the election," Miyatake replied.

"Are you going to change the election?"

"I sure as hell am gonna try."

Miyatake later said that at that point his connection with Peggy Maze became stronger. He would have voted for Cunningham, he said, had the incumbent not changed his mind; now he campaigned vigorously for Lowry. Miyatake worked particularly hard to send out letters to the Chinese community: "If Cunningham isn't going to support this for Japanese Americans, what do you think he's gonna do for you?"[8] Lowry won the election by a little more than 3,000 votes.

The media, by and large, were very supportive of redress, or at least of the upcoming Day of Remembrance. And, with Lowry's election, some SERC and Day of Remembrance activists were wondering where the backlash was. It seemed to many of these activists that the largest noticeable backlash was coming not from Euroamericans but from Japanese Americans fearful of once again triggering anti-Japanese emotions. Aki Kurose, organizer of the potluck, recalled:

> I had one friend saying, "I'm not going to go. Why should we all gather there?" And she said, "They'll say, 'This is a Jap invasion.'" And so there were some that were fearful of a reunion. . . . I said, "Come on, let's go." And she said, "I'm not gonna be one of the Buddhaheads." . . . She really had a hard time dealing with it.[9]

Writers, visual artists, and performing artists were included in the program along with politicians, judges, scholars, and civic leaders, to ensure true community representation; the whole idea was to give the event the flavor of a community outing. But Chin did not want any Japanese American speakers on redress. Although the organizing had to be done by Nisei and Issei, and although the Nikkei community had to be out front, Chin believed that redress would be mentioned by politicians, especially if they had agreed to speak at a gathering like this one.

"Can't have any Japanese Americans complaining on TV," Chin said. "Let the white politicians do that. They'll do it. They know what this is about. The Japanese Americans need only to talk about their experiences."

So Chin reasoned. This policy was to become a sticking point with the national JACL leaders.

In the days leading up to the Day of Remembrance, the newspapers in Seattle, Tacoma, Auburn, Bellevue, and local neighborhoods ran major articles on the event. These articles featured interviews with former internees who now lived in the papers' circulation areas. Many of the news releases quoted Sasaki and Miyatake. The press coverage was no accident. Frank Chin, Frank Abe, and Kathy Wong had put a lot of effort into the press kits. Chin believed that the local press would pick up the fact that "the DOR would signal a major cultural shift in our community," and that although "the Nisei still felt scarred by the Hearst press of the 1940s, a new generation of editors and reporters had grown up and was ready to tell the story our way."[10]

Excitement built as everything began to fall into place. Gov. Dan Evans, Seattle Mayor Charles Royer, and the Seattle City Council sent their endorsements. The Nisei Veterans Committee arranged for the color guard and National Guard trucks to carry former internees back to Puyallup. Still, no one knew how many would show up on the day itself.

RETURN TO CAMP HARMONY

> It has taken us a long time to get here. The journey has been hazardous, has been long. But we have come here on our own. . . . Throw open the gates! Tear down the fences! Let all be fair on the grounds!
>
> —Lawson Inada[11]

Chin looked around nervously as he drove to the parking lot of Sick's Stadium, in Seattle.[12] No one he had talked with had any idea of how many people would show up; 500 max, Chin thought. He was also worried about Lowry, who had told him that he couldn't join the caravan to Puyallup because of a prior commitment.

"Be there," Chin told him, "at least at the Sick's Stadium parking lot. You promised you'd be there." Chin felt that politicians' attendance was critical to legitimizing the event: if Lowry backed out, what would others do?

As the stadium parking lot came into view, Chin panicked: it looked like an RV trailer show. What is this? he thought. Where are all the Japanese Americans?

Then he noticed that they were there, lots of them, and so was Lowry. Bullhorn in hand, he was booming out from the back of a truck, calling the World War II internment "a tragic mistake." His appearance, he said, was "a small testimonial toward righting a wrong."[13]

As the community continued to gather in the parking lot, the people who were to participate in the caravan to Puyallup were provided with yellow tags, replicas of the ones the internees had been forced to put on in 1942 when they gathered for their trip to the assembly centers. The Day of Remembrance participants were told to write their names and "family numbers" on the tags. At the bottom of each yellow tag were the words TO BE ATTACHED TO HAND BAGGAGES CARRIED BY PERSON, but people attached the tags to their lapels, just as many had done decades before.

The turnout surprised participants and organizers alike. More than 2,000 people had come to Sick's Stadium. Sam Shoji, at the wheel of the first civilian vehicle in the caravan to Puyallup, said that the sight of everyone driving down the freeway was nothing short of "awesome." Cherry Kinoshita agreed: "I never dreamed of the extent to which the community would turn out for the event. The endless caravan of cars, two miles long, wending down the freeway with lights on and police escorts, was one of the most impressive sights I can recall."[14]

Chin describes the atmosphere and emotions of November 25:

> In family cars, tucked into the caravan rolling slowly from an abandoned baseball stadium in Seattle, down I-5, off at Exit 142-B, following the signs to Puyallup, Nisei who had promised never to go back and had never talked of camp to their Sansei children when they were children, when they were in high school, when they were in college, when they lived at home, started talking now. Families had gone into the camps. Families had not come out. Today, families went in, and took over, and families would come out, joined by the realization that the fear, the doubts, humiliation and anxiety that isolated family members from each other, and families from families, were shared in common by all who lived through the evacuation and camps. The suffering each carried was no longer suspected of being a personal mental illness, and the burden of suffering and bitterness was lifted at the return to Camp Harmony. The atmosphere was more picnic than political and the feeling all around was downright affectionate.[15]

The day was an unforgettable moment in Japanese American history, let alone in the redress campaign. Memories of 1942 were shared by Monica Sone, who read selections from her book *Nisei Daughter,* which chronicles her 1940s childhood in Seattle and in camp. The actor Pat Morita recalled that camp food consisted of U.S. Army quartermaster rejects, and Sasaki read an excerpt from his diary, describing the day he and his sister's family left for Camp Harmony:

My sister was there, standing with her family's baggage with her two children. One was a baby of four months, the other a child not quite three. In the confusion of the departure from her home, my sister had failed to bring an umbrella and was badly struggling to shield her children from the drizzle.

Suddenly, the door of the house adjacent to where my sister was standing opened and, to my sister's surprise, she and her children were invited by the madam [of a brothel] into the parlor for protection from the rain.

By that display of pity and compassion toward a stranger and her children on their way to exile, that white madam demonstrated a kindness of heart and absence of racism that the rest of Seattle did not appear to possess on that dismal morning.[16]

Other speakers included the actor Mako; Charles Z. Smith, then a professor at the University of Washington; Gordon Hirabayashi, a sociology professor at the University of Washington, who was well known for defying the eviction and curfew laws during World War II, and whose challenge to these laws became a Supreme Court case; and Amy Uno Ishii, sister of one of the first redress thinkers, the late Edison Uno. According to an article published the following day in *The Daily Journal-American*, there was also a talent show featuring "tap dancers, a young woman performing an aria from *Madame Butterfly*, [and] a young man who turned the old cowboy tune, 'Don't Fence Me In,' into a political statement."[17]

People at this first Day of Remembrance could also view arts and crafts that had been made in camp, as well as the original *Pride and Shame* exhibit. Tours of the former camp site, *odori* (dance) performances, a slide show on Minidoka, and a Japanese American play, *Lady Is Dying*, added to the celebration of the day that allowed more than 2,000 Japanese Americans to remember a history that many had said they would prefer to forget.

"It was the largest gathering of Japanese Americans since the camps," the poet Lawson Inada observed.[18] For Japanese Americans, the constitutionally guaranteed right of assembly had been suspended since December 1941: although it was the United States government that originally imposed the ban on gathering in large numbers, the Day of Remembrance made Japanese Americans realize that they had been internalizing the ban for 37 years. In a place where many of the participants had once been imprisoned, the "Jap invasion" (as Aki Kurose's friend feared the DOR would be perceived) became a joyous and powerful reawakening.

The explosive energy of the Day of Remembrance served to energize communities all along the West Coast. The media coverage was overwhelmingly supportive, despite ABC's ultimate decision, after filming the whole event, not to run the *20/20* segment.[19] Within a week, Oregonians who had attended the Puyallup gathering were discussing the possibility of mounting a Day of Remembrance in Portland; Jim Tsujimura, Bones Onishi, and other Portland organizers enlisted Chin, Abe, and Wong to help organize it. By the end of the year, several other West Coast cities with large Japanese American communities were planning Days of Remembrance, most aiming for February 19, 1979, and some aiming for March and April. None of these gatherings matched the attendance of the Seattle DOR, but Portland's DOR, held at the Livestock Exposition Center, was nearly as successful. Chin, Abe, and Wong were able to involve the various factions in the community, attracting 1,500 people to the event.

Nevertheless, the success of the Day of Remembrance brought SERC's rift with the national JACL to the forefront. JACL's National Committee for Redress felt that it had been slighted at Puyallup. In addition, the committee, reacting to increased publicity, some of it unfavorable, about redress, and to advice from Sen. Daniel Inouye of Hawaii, began to explore other options for redress. A letter from National Committee for Redress chair John Tateishi to Ron Mamiya, then one of two committee members from Seattle, complimented the organizers on the Day of Remembrance but emphasized Tateishi's (and perhaps media chair Ellen Endo's) unhappiness with the DOR program:

> As I mentioned to you, I felt that the program of speakers very strongly gave the impression that the Redress campaign is a local issue involving primarily the Seattle area. I have absolutely no objection to the event itself being a local one (which I think is only right), but if the ABC cameras are to be limited to what went on at Puyallup, I'm concerned that a lot of people across the country will get the impression that Redress is a regional concern and not one that concerns the entire country and involves a national organization. Whatever else some people may feel about the JACL, the fact remains that JACL will carry the burden of the campaign and will be the organization that will fight to get a bill through Congress. This fact, I feel, was completely lost in the program.
>
> I don't think recognition and credit for JACL are important in them-

selves just for recognition and credit, but I do think it's important that the American public understand that a national civil rights / advocacy organization is behind the push for redress.

I know that you weren't responsible for determining the line-up of speakers, but again, let me give you my thoughts on this. When the Camp Harmony planning group requested funding from the Redress budget and support from National Headquarters, I felt that we should back you in any way possible. Consequently, I arranged for the funding and talked both Clifford [Uyeda, national JACL president] and Karl [Nobuyuki, the JACL national director] into going to Puyallup for the event. To be completely frank with you, I was upset that neither Karl nor Clifford [was] invited to speak to the audience and felt that they were virtually ignored. At the least, I felt that both of them should have been placed on the agenda of speakers as representatives of the National JACL.

This [harks] back to my earlier point, but I think it's an extremely important one and what it comes down to is this: if we're going to achieve any degree of success in Redress, we're going to have to work as a team through the national organization and machinery of JACL. This issue is too important to screw it up through ignoring the national organization. There are no heroes in the Redress campaign: we either make it together or we don't make it at all.[20]

Chin and Miyatake, of course, had made the decision not to have any Japanese Americans speak on redress, whether from the Seattle redress movement or the national JACL. Because of that decision, the tension between the two groups continued to build.

"JAPANESE AMERICANS' PUBLIC ENEMY NO. 1"

The people who push this regard me as Public Enemy No. 1. But don't forget that I speak for probably—no one has made a statistical survey—a majority of Japanese Americans.

—Sen. S. I. Hayakawa[21]

Redress had become a newsworthy issue after the 1978 JACL convention in Salt Lake City and the Days of Remembrance on the West Coast, but back in Washington, D.C., a U.S. senator of Japanese ancestry, elected from California, was becoming one of the most vocal opponents of redress and causing the issue to take on greater significance in the media. The comments of S. I. Hayakawa were getting a lot of print and air time and were beginning to anger redress advocates. Hayakawa, born a Canadian, had spent the war years in Chicago and had not been evicted or incarcerated. His statements—that the camps had been merely "relocation centers" and "safe refuges" from vigilantes on the West Coast, and that they had been "the best thing that could have happened" to Japanese Americans—were offensive to those who had spent time behind barbed wire. Hayakawa pursued his anti-redress platform with claims that the War Relocation Authority had "encouraged" internees to leave camp during the day. Such statements created controversy, which the media loved.[22]

In Hayakawa's remarks the Day of Remembrance steering committee saw another opportunity to further the cause of redress. To answer the California senator, the committee decided to run an ad in the *Washington Post.* Frank Chin drafted an open letter to the senator, and the committee, led by Frank Abe and Karen Seriguchi, began to drum up national-level support and donations for the ad.[23] At Days of Remembrance held up and down the West Coast, the committee set up tables and collected money and signatures for the open letter. Supporters were asked to send their donations to David Ishii, the antiquarian bookseller who had allowed his store to be used as the headquarters for the DOR steering committee. Donations of $1, $5, $10, and $20 were accompanied by expressions of anger toward Hayakawa, and many supporters sent letters to publications that had printed his anti-redress comments. As "Kats" Nishimura wrote to the *Washington Post,* for example,

> Please don't let the color of his skin fool you into thinking that he [Hayakawa] speaks for the rest of us. He was elected to office by an overwhelming majority of ultra-conservative *haoles* [Caucasians] which seeks to buy his yellow skin and white heart to betray the oppressed minorities.[24]

Some questioned Hayakawa's sanity, logic, and motives. Others—like Walter M. Weglyn, a Jewish American who had once "suffered the savagery that Hitlerian demagoguery brought about"—responded to Hayakawa's games with semantics. Weglyn, challenging the senator's statement that the redress movement, by using such terms as *concentration camps,* "trivializes the massacre of those millions of Jews," wrote:

> So now you want to pit Jews against Japanese Americans. What next? . . . Yes, *concentration camps*—barbed wire fencing, guard towers and all—on

howling wasteland areas in this land of "liberty and justice for all." Your belaboring the semantic "accuracy" of calling them "relocation centers" is pure sophistry.[25]

Many also responded with simple messages of support. For example, a young girl wrote, "My name is Mia Hayashida. I am 11 years old and I go to North Mercer Junior High. I am contributing $2.00 allowance money and wish it could have been more."[26]

The open letter ran in the *Washington Post* on May 9, 1979, with hundreds of names signed at the bottom. Because of a typesetting deadline space limitations, an additional 600 names, mostly those of Sansei and Yonsei, had to be omitted. With the support of a wide range of people—the writers Jeanne Wakatsuki Houston and Hisaye Yamamoto De Soto; Gordon Hirabayashi and Min Yasui, defendants in two of the original test cases; such friends of redress as the actress Jane Fonda, the poet and publisher Lawrence Ferlinghetti, the journalist Studs Terkel, and the mayors of Seattle, Portland, and San Francisco; and many members of JACL's National Committee for Redress— the open letter was a powerful statement. "You, Senator Hayakawa, were not there with us," the letter declared, after a short historical summation of the forced evacuation:

> *After camp we had nothing.* That nothing is what camp gave us, not opportunity. It was hard work, combined with the help of a few good friends, that brought us our present success. That success does not make the concentration camps of yesterday any less heinous a violation of American justice. Our success does not excuse the camps from American history.
>
> What you call the white hysteria of the time does not excuse or lessen the damage done to Japanese America or American justice. . . .
>
> In camp we maintained our faith in the justice of a nation that had broken faith with us. Our all-Nisei 442nd Regimental Combat Team fought in WWII with a distinction that made them the most decorated of any unit who fought in that awful war. With that same faith in American justice, we seek redress. What you have said about white backlash and forgetting the hardships we endured convince[s] us that—unless the concentration camps become a recognized and essential part of American history—our ideals and system are vulnerable to the very tyranny Americans loathe. The concentration camps can happen again.[27]

The open letter also generated much media attention for redress and the DOR steering committee. Press conferences were held in Seattle, San Francisco, Chicago, and Los Angeles, keeping the issue of redress in the news.

The wide support for the open letter demonstrated that Hayakawa's anti-redress stance was one issue on which many could agree. But the Seattle Chapter JACL and the DOR steering committee would continue to learn that redress positions were not all cut from the same mold. As the DOR committee raised money to print the open letter to Hayakawa, alternative redress moves were being considered by some members of JACL's National Committee for Redress.

4 / Circumvention

> At the meeting of the National Committee for Redress held December
> 9–10, it was decided that we would submit a Redress bill during the cur-
> rent session of the United States Congress. Predicated on this schedule,
> we have worked out the initial plans for our Redress strategy.
>
> —John Tateishi[1]

At its December 1978 meeting, the JACL National Committee for Redress
decided that Ron Mamiya and John Tateishi should go to Washington, D.C.,
to discuss redress proposals with the Nikkei members of Congress.[2]

On January 30, 1979, national JACL representatives met with Sens. Daniel
Inouye and Spark Matsunaga, both of Hawaii, and Reps. Norman Mineta
and Robert Matsui, both of California, to discuss "possible alternatives vis-
à-vis methodology for a redress bill to be introduced to the United States
Congress."[3] The idea, according to Tateishi, was to find out the Nikkei congressional delegation's thoughts on legislative redress. Two plans were presented to the delegation: the Seattle plan (or tax-checkoff plan, as some called
it), developed by Henry Miyatake and the Seattle Evacuation Redress
Committee, and the national JACL alternative, the direct-appropriations plan,
developed by the national JACL and JACL's National Committee for Redress.

Reps. Mineta and Matsui raised concerns over the Seattle plan, saying it
would draw too much attention to itself and create the possibility of a backlash. Mineta also pointed out that the IRS was in the middle of trying to "sim-
plify the tax form," and the Seattle plan would run counter to this effort. Sen.
Matsunaga was intrigued with the tax-checkoff proposal—specifically, the
potential it held for the education of the general public—but Inouye felt that
the plan was a bad idea because, as Tateishi reported, "it would possibly
encourage other minority groups to seek compensation for past injustices."

A plan of this sort, Sen. Inouye said, would also have to go through the House Ways and Means Committee, where it was unlikely to succeed. He added that he thought there would be only one chance to seek redress through Congress, and "for this reason, we must give a great deal of thought to the type of legislation we introduce." According to Tateishi, Inouye

> also stated that there is no question that we were treated unjustly by the American government and that we are completely justified in seeking Redress. However, he expressed the view that, while $25,000 is in no way adequate as compensation for what we suffered, $3 billion would never be acceptable to the Congress of the United States. With this in mind, he recommended that we consider introducing a bill which would establish a Congressional commission to study the Redress issue. The advantage of such a commission would be that, on the one hand, it would lend credibility to Redress if the recommendation of the commission were in our favor, and also that the commission would lay the preliminary groundwork for introduction of a Redress bill to the Congress. . . . A question of introducing concurrently a number of Redress bills was raised, to which Senators Inouye and Matsunaga and Congressman Mineta felt that such a strategy is inadvisable because it would give the impression that our efforts are not unified. This would be important in addressing Congress, especially since Japanese Americans make up such a small percentage of the general population.

After a month of deliberations about the advice that had been offered by the Nikkei congressional delegation, the National Redress Committee met on March 3, 1979, and formally endorsed, by a vote of 4 to 2, " 'the concept of a congressional commission to the exclusion of any other redress plan.' The congressional commission would determine the extent of the injuries sustained by persons of Japanese ancestry in our evacuation / internment, whether those injuries should be redressed, and the method of such redress, if any." The two voting against the commission idea were from Seattle: Henry Miyatake and Ron Mamiya.[4]

As a lawyer and chair of the legislative subcommittee for redress, Mamiya had the task of preparing the legislation for presentation to Congress. He had volunteered for the assignment in August 1978, shortly after JACL's national convention in Salt Lake City, when there was very little talk of a congressional commission. Mamiya was not interested in preparing legislation that called for congressional hearings instead of redress: he stated in a letter to Tateishi, JACL president Clifford Uyeda, and vice president Jim Tsujimura that he could not, "in good faith and conscience" do so "without further clarification."⁵ Mamiya felt that the vote had gone against the mandates established by the JACL National Council at the previous four national conventions, and he asked for clarification of the committee's vote as well as for an explanation of "how a Congressional Commission falls within the Salt Lake City National Convention mandate." In addition, he called on Tateishi, Uyeda, and Tsujimura to reconsider the decision, stating that Japanese Americans should "not allow our Government to dictate what we want and what is best for us."⁶

Tateishi quickly fired off a response, saying that it was important for Mamiya to "remember that the decision was made by the committee as a body and not by individual fiat. In this regard, the discussion of the issue was held in committee, and as a committee, we will stick to it." He continued:

> I cannot, in all honesty, take lightly your own personal decision to contravene the adjuration of the committee to develop the draft and final product of the legislation as quickly as possible. From my perspective as the chair of the committee, you have violated a critical responsibility entrusted to you and indeed requested by you, and have subordinated a decision of the committee to your own personal doubts. I find this totally unacceptable and would direct a similar criticism towards any committee member under similar circumstances.
>
> In view of this, I feel that it is necessary for me to relieve you of your responsibility as the chair of the legislative subcommittee and as a member of JACL's National Committee for Redress. Given the critical timing we're under and the nature of the circumstances, you leave me very little choice in this matter.⁷

At its March 21 meeting, the Seattle Chapter JACL board responded to Tateishi's firing of Mamiya with a unanimous vote to support Mamiya's request for clarification, and it commended him for "taking a stand on a difficult issue." Moreover, like Mamiya, the Seattle Chapter JACL also asked for clarification of how the National Redress Committee's decision to pursue a congressional commission fell within the mandate that had been set by the JACL National Council during the 1978 convention in Salt Lake City.⁸ The chapter reasoned that the Salt Lake City convention had mandated a redress bill, not an investigative body that would determine whether redress was justified. The facts of the case were known to legal scholars and historians, and of course to the Japanese American community; to dig out facts that were already known was simply a waste of time, the chapter thought, and was certain to deprive aging Issei of their payments should a redress bill later pass.

At the end of April, Tateishi sent a letter to Henry Miyatake, asking whether he supported the commission approach. If not, Tateishi wrote, "I don't see how, in good conscience and with honesty, you can choose to remain as a member of the National Committee for Redress."[9] But Miyatake never saw the letter. When a copy was shown to him years later, he took one look at the date and said, "That was the period my divorce trial was going on."

In a March 24, 1979, letter to all the JACL chapter presidents, Seattle Chapter JACL president Mich Matsudaira presented the Seattle chapter's point of view, and he urged all chapters to speak out about redress because, he said, the national JACL would be more concerned about testimony given to the proposed commission than about plans for redress. The national JACL responded at its June 2 national board meeting, voting 13 to 1, with 2 abstentions, to support the National Redress Committee's decision to prepare a commission bill. In addition, Tateishi asked the board to conduct a poll of the entire membership via the chapters. The board complied.[10]

Of all the JACL chapters, only the Seattle chapter opposed the commission bill. On July 20, 1979, the Seattle Chapter JACL board voted unanimously against the commission approach.[11] All the JACL district councils, including the Pacific Northwest District Council, backed the National Committee for Redress. By late July, it appeared not only that the national JACL would go forward with the commission bill but also that the bill would pass.

S. 1647, a bill to establish the Commission on Wartime Relocation and Internment of Civilians (CWRIC), was introduced in the U.S. Senate on August 2 by Sens. Inouye and Matsunaga, Sens. Frank Church and James McClure of Idaho, and Sens. Alan Cranston and S. I. Hayakawa of California. Many were surprised by Hayakawa's "conversion," but, as JACL executive director Karl Nobuyuki pointed out, CWRIC was not a "redress" bill.[12] In September, the CWRIC bill was introduced in the House of Representatives as H.R. 5499.[13]

A SHORT-LIVED ROMANCE

In mid-May, shortly after the open letter to Hayakawa ran in the *Washington Post*, and while the national JACL was going ahead with its commission bill,

William Hohri, a member of the Chicago JACL chapter's Redress Committee, took a weekend trip to Seattle to meet with SERC activists. Henry Miyatake, Shosuke Sasaki, and Chuck Kato greeted Hohri and laid out their plan for redress. They asked Hohri if he would be interested in assuming leadership of the redress campaign.[14]

SERC was in a quandary. Its members felt they had to keep their momentum going, especially since Rep. Mike Lowry would be introducing a redress bill. They also believed that only a national organization could carry a bill through Congress. But if JACL and the Nikkei members of Congress were going to avoid confronting the redress issue directly, then perhaps a national redress organization had to be created. The Chicago JACL chapter's Redress Committee had been outspoken in its opposition to the commission bill, and Miyatake, Sasaki, and Kato felt that a Chicagoan would have more clout than anyone in Seattle. They also felt that Hohri "was independent of, but not unfriendly towards, the JACL."[15]

The day after his meeting with the three SERC activists, Hohri met with other activists, among them Frank Abe, Ron Mamiya, Tomio Moriguchi, Ken Nakano, Karen Seriguchi, and Kathy Wong. At that meeting, the National Council for Japanese American Redress (NCJAR) was formed. Hohri, feeling slightly uncomfortable about leading a group founded in Seattle, did not agree at that time to become its leader, but two weeks later he did.[16]

In the following months, the Day of Remembrance steering committee and SERC (with overlapping membership) worked together with Lowry aides Ruthann Kurose and Kathy Halley to draft the Lowry bill. By November 1979, however, the Seattle NCJAR members had begun to drift apart from Hohri.

The dispute, according to Miyatake, was over topics being discussed in the NCJAR newsletter, one issue of which included an article about atrocities committed in Manchuria by the Japanese. These articles angered Sasaki because he felt that what the Japanese government did had nothing to do with Japanese American redress. Miyatake also felt that Hohri needed to clear articles with the whole group before printing them. Hohri had a different perception of the rift, blaming it on a difference in opinion over the tax-checkoff method of funding redress, which he called "clever, perhaps, too clever":

> The [tax-checkoff] plan tried to avoid an issue which should not be avoided: the liability of citizens for the actions of their government. If the

government did commit serious wrongs, then the citizenry should make amends. . . . Although the dispute over funding can be described neatly on paper, it took place between individuals and did create a breach between redress supporters in Seattle and those in Chicago.[17]

Despite the national JACL's decision to go ahead with the commission bill, the Seattle chapter decided to push ahead with Rep. Lowry's promise to introduce a redress bill. The draft of Lowry's bill called for the sum of $10,000, plus $15 per day of incarceration, to be paid to eligible persons, and, according to Miyatake, eligible persons, as defined by SERC, "covered everybody . . . including Germans, Indians, Italians, everybody that was affected by the government, not just the E.O. 9066, but the coverage by some of the other resolutions, executive orders that were put out for the Eastern seaboard. That was a separate sector altogether. Those people were affected."

Miyatake felt strongly that all these groups had been subject to the unfair application of the law, especially the Aleuts, whom he had met in Alaska while working for the Federal Aviation Administration from 1948 to 1951:

> I used to fly from Anchorage down the Aleutian chain to all these different places, down to Kiska and Shemya. And these places used to have Aleutian natives, and you get into discussions: "Well, you know, during the war, they took us off the islands, and they separated me from my family, and they put my family into little cannery places, and they put me in the road gang, and I had to work." I said, "What did they do that for?" He says, "I don't know. They just round us all up." . . . They did more things brutally to those people than they did to us. They separated the males from the rest of their family. . . . So a lot of this other stuff was in the back of my mind. So I was trying to do an all-encompassed coverage kind of thing.

Miyatake also felt that broad coverage would help passage of the bill, because it would gain more supporters. The drafters of Lowry's bill apparently thought otherwise, however: when H.R. 5977 was introduced, the only individuals covered by its provisions were people of Japanese ancestry who had been interned, detained, or forcibly relocated by the United States.

Another change made from the SERC draft was the method of funding. H.R. 5977 replaced the tax-checkoff plan with a direct appropriation. There were problems with the tax-checkoff method simply because any tax-based bill would have had to jump through many more hoops. Others also did not like it, and for the very reason why Mike Nakata thought it was brilliant: it seemed as if Japanese Americans were being asked to pay for their own redress. But the amount of $10,000 plus $15 per day of incarceration, as well as the designation of who would receive payments first, remained intact.

A provision proposed by Shosuke Sasaki—that it was the responsibility of the government to find all the eligible evacuees and internees—also was retained. SERC felt that it was important for eligible recipients not to have to apply and that the government should have all necessary records. H.R. 5977 stipulated that the attorney general "shall locate, as soon as practicable after the date of the enactment of this Act, each eligible individual."

In November 1979, Lowry, with 24 co-sponsors, introduced his redress bill. House Speaker Tip O'Neill referred H.R. 5977 to the Judiciary Committee. Lowry, answering critics who charged that H.R. 5977 would hurt the chances of passing the commission bill, said, "It's just the opposite. I think the commission bill will pass. It has a lot of supporters, but I think the redress bill will help. . . . The purpose of my bill is to introduce the concept of reparations into the hearings so people begin to think about the possibility. . . . "[18]

The importance of Lowry's bill was not lost on his constituents. At a time when Japanese American political leaders were unwilling to openly support redress payments to individuals, because they thought it would be political suicide, an Irish American introduced this bill because he saw the World War II expulsion as a violation of fundamental constitutional rights. As Lowry said,

> I don't see how it's possible that reasonable men could look at the facts and not come to the conclusion that a great injustice was done and that some meaningful legislation is necessary to correct that act. There is strong sentiment in Congress to let people know about what happened in 1942 and to pass some meaningful legislation. They remember how bad it was and want to do something about it.[19]

According to Lowry, "It would [have been] tougher politically for an American of Japanese ancestry than it would be for somebody like [Rep.] Barney Frank or Mike Lowry, who were not. And it takes somebody to go out there first."[20] Lowry aide Ruthann Kurose also pointed out that Lowry had "introduced [the bill] as a civil liberties issue," and that the bill would have run the risk of being seen as a Japanese American–only issue if a Nikkei representative had introduced it. Lowry, asked what part H.R. 5977 had played in the final redress bill that passed in 1988, replied that his bill

> established that redress had to include individual payment. There had to be individual compensation for individual rights denied. . . . There really was not anything approaching an adequate addressing of this terrible violation of our Constitution. There wasn't individual compensation and it wasn't that people receiving compensation cared about the money. That's [the] only way you address it: redress this type of constitutional violation. . . . People could argue forever as to whether it should be $5,000 or $100,000 or how it works down through the heirs or anything else. The important principle was there was going to be individual compensation. And once that had been established, there wasn't any moving back from that.[21]

During the early part of 1980, SERC worked on Lowry's bill. With the commission bill getting the full backing of the national JACL and the Nikkei congressional delegation, however, the forces arrayed against the Seattle redress group were too much to overcome. In effect, the battle over the competing bills, one for a commission and the other for direct appropriations, confirmed what Miyatake and Nakata had felt all along: that it would take a national organization to get a bill through Congress.

S. 1647, the commission bill, was amended in the Senate Committee on Governmental Affairs to include investigation of the expulsion of Aleuts from their homes during World War II, and to grant the committee subpoena powers. The amended bill passed the Senate with very little controversy on May 22, 1980.[22]

The House Judiciary Committee held hearings for H.R. 5499 (the House bill to establish a commission) and H.R. 5977 (Lowry's bill) on June 2. Only Lowry himself and William Hohri, representing the National Council for Japanese American Redress, testified in support of Lowry's bill. John Tateishi, representing JACL, and Mike Masaoka (see chap. 2), representing the Nisei Lobby, testified in support of the commission bill.[23] Lowry's bill died in committee, but H.R. 5499 was passed out of committee, and it passed in Congress on July 21, 1980. On July 31, to coincide with the national JACL convention, President Jimmy Carter signed the commission bill into law,[24] and the Commission on Wartime Relocation and Internment of Civilians was established. Its directives were clear:

To review the facts and circumstances surrounding Executive Order Numbered 9066, issued February 19, 1942, and the impact of such Executive Order on American citizens and permanent resident aliens; to review directives of U.S. military forces requiring the relocation and, in some cases, detention in internment camps of American citizens, including Aleut civilians, and permanent resident aliens of the Aleutian and Pribilof Islands; and to recommend appropriate remedies.[25]

5 / Testimony

Your Honor, I don't want you to misunderstand me. I certainly do not begrudge the fact the Commission exists. That's why I am here today, to bring this information on the popular support for redress.

—Frank Abe[1]

One day we were free citizens, residents of communities, law abiding, protective of our families, and proud. The next day we were inmates of cramped, crowded American style concentration camps, under armed guards, fed like prisoners in mess hall lines, deprived of privacy and dignity, and shorn of all our rights. In the Portland Exposition Center there were 3,600 people under one roof. The horses' stalls were made into living quarters, and in the exhibition area plywood sheets made up the four walls of the family units. . . . In the corner were four folded army cots. We were told that mattresses would be provided for us. The "mattresses" turned out to be a bag made of ticking which was to be filled with hay. It was the most depressing period of my life. I never expected that this country, where I was born, would treat me in this manner. . . .

—Emi Somekawa[2]

The members of the close-knit Seattle Evacuation Redress Committee began to drift apart after Lowry's bill had been passed over in favor of the Commission on Wartime Relocation and Internment of Civilians. There was a general sense that the whole momentum for redress had been stalled by the national JACL and the Nikkei members of the U.S. Congress. In addition, Henry Miyatake, who for almost ten years had provided much of the driving energy for the Seattle movement, was confronting the unexpected death of his son, a crippling injury to his daughter, and divorce proceedings. Faced with difficult times in his personal life, he contributed minimally to the post-1980 redress movement in Seattle.

Chuck Kato and Ken Nakano continued to work with the national JACL's plan, feeling that JACL's route was the only game in town. As for the commission, "sometimes you win, sometimes you lose," Nakano thought; "you just don't quit because you lose."[3] Both men also felt a certain loyalty to and respect for Cherry Kinoshita, who would emerge as a key player, both nationally and locally, in the drive for redress.

In camp, Kinoshita, with "a smattering of high school journalism," had worked for the *Minidoka Irrigator*. After working at the *Irrigator* for a while, she was assigned to write a column about such "light things" as "what do you do with your hairstyle when the dust is blowing, and all that kind of silly stupid stuff."[4] But in "Feminidoka," as her column was titled, Kinoshita did not always write about beauty tips:

> Once I sat down to do a column and it was going to be a reminiscing—because, you know, we had been there maybe a year—and I was reminiscing about our past and I was going to write this little light article. And I looked at the typewriter and I thought, really, what is so great about this life? So that's when I wrote the column [about] the dust, the cold, and the bitterness, but the worst thing of all was the lack of freedom. That we could not go out, you know; we couldn't go as we pleased and here we were. And it ended—somebody sent me that column later and I didn't realize what I had said—it ended something like, we are birds in a cage. So that's when it really hit me that, you know, here we are prisoners. We are prisoners and we hadn't done anything wrong.[5]

The memory of that moment, Kinoshita later explained, would help push her on in the struggle for redress.

Kinoshita had first been exposed to the idea of redress at the national JACL convention in 1970, where, she remembered, Edison Uno had made his plea for action. By the mid-1970s, she had become a Seattle Chapter JACL officer and was drawn into the redress movement by the impassioned stance of SERC, whose members convinced her that individual payments were a necessary part of redress.

"Apology, fine," she would later say. "You know, we need that, but you need monetary compensation to back that up because—and the phrase that sticks in my mind is "our American system of justice"—you don't go to court and say you've been wronged or damaged. There is always a monetary award."[6] She also explained:

> Somehow, I think 18 year olds were more naive in [1942] and we accepted, I think, . . . what is the phrase? Power of authority. Obedience to authority . . . that was very strong, particularly in our culture. And you still listen to the government; I mean, you did whatever the government said. There wasn't that feeling of rebellion except for a few. . . . [7]

By the early 1980s, Kinoshita's participation, as she might modestly have called her involvement in the redress movement, would be described by others as nothing less than wholehearted leadership. She had been in San Francisco for the national JACL convention when President Carter signed the commission bill. On the flight back to Seattle, Kinoshita decided to convene a meeting of Japanese American community organizations, to secure Seattle as one of the sites of the commission hearings. The members of the community also needed to prepare to testify about their wartime experiences. To facilitate both goals, Kinoshita met with Gordon Hirabayashi, Chuck Kato, Henry Miyatake, Tomio Moriguchi, Karen Seriguchi, and Emi Somekawa on August 15, 1980.

The others agreed with Kinoshita that a community-wide, volunteer redress organization was necessary, and in September it was established, with Hirabayashi and Kinoshita as co-chairs and Karen Seriguchi as secretary-treasurer. Led by the redress committee of Seattle Chapter JACL, and calling itself the Community Committee on Redress / Reparations (CCRR), it included representatives from the other three area JACL chapters (Puyallup, White River, and Lake Washington), seven churches with predominantly Japanese American congregations (Blaine Methodist, Nichiren Buddhist, Seattle Betsuin, St. Peter's Episcopal, Japanese Baptist, Faith Bible, Japanese Presbyterian), the Nisei Veterans Committee, the Nikkeijinkai (a community service organization), and Nikkei Concerns.[8] The co-chairs decided to split up the tasks to be done, with Kinoshita taking on the "grunt work." Hirabayashi, well known for his defiance of the eviction and curfew laws during World War II, lent his name to the committee and spoke before many groups, actively drumming up support for and awareness of the redress campaign.[9] Once Seattle had been informed of its selection as a site for the commission hearings, the committee worked feverishly to prepare local Nikkei citizens who wished to testify about their experiences during World War II.

Chuck Kato has called Seriguchi one of the most important figures in the Seattle redress story:

> She set up talks with various school classes, including high schools, colleges, [and] junior highs, and had speakers such as myself and others. She got us on talk shows and TV to refute the people like Lillian Baker and other "red necks" who never will understand the real meaning of the Constitution of the U.S. The people of Seattle really owe a lot to Karen, and when she left . . . it was as if we lost a "right arm". . . . [10]

By February 1981, knowing that the commission was gathering data and possible witnesses, CCRR had developed a survey that was sent out to 9,000 people through the mailing lists of local organizations. The letter that accompanied the survey stated:

> We hope that the hearings will generate a new record of the many aspects of the internment and its effects on our lives. The U.S. government has never before conducted an inquiry into this matter, and the hearing presents a once-in-a-lifetime opportunity to tell our story.
>
> Thus we ask your assistance in identifying potential witnesses among your family, friends, church, or community group. Some of the things people could testify about are: economic losses, loss of health, emotional suffering, damage to family structure, the need for redress. [11]

By March, 851 surveys had been returned, and 50 of the respondents volunteered to give testimony. The survey asked respondents which form of redress they wanted. The results showed that 36 percent preferred monetary compensation to be paid only to individuals, 7 percent preferred a trust fund to be used only for community development, and 58 percent wanted the funds to go both to individuals and to the community. [12] After Seriguchi reported the survey results to the JACL Pacific Northwest District Council, the Spokane and Portland JACL chapters requested the forms so that they could conduct their own surveys and identify volunteer witnesses. The Puyallup chapter also conducted a survey of its local area. In addition to the 3,500 households reached in the Seattle area, an estimated 1,500 or more households were surveyed by those three JACL chapters. [13]

Workshops on the commission hearings had begun as early as December

1980, with CCRR's workshop on handling the media, where Seriguchi, Abe (by then a radio journalist at KIRO), and Evelyn Iritani of the *Seattle Times* gave pointers on responding to questions that the media would be most likely to ask—questions like "Why all this concern about redress 38 years after the war?" and "What comes to mind when you think of the camps?" and "Don't you feel that going to camp was your patriotic duty? After all, everybody sacrifices during wartime." These workshops helped get the participants focused months before the mainstream media began covering the preparations for the hearings.[14]

The workshops continued from late January through May 1981. For example, CCRR organized a community meeting with Hugh Burnton Mitchell, former U.S. senator from Washington and now a CWRIC commissioner, and Professor Roger Daniels to give community members an opportunity to talk with experts about the hearing process.[15] Because the commission would be accepting both written and oral testimony, two workshops were also scheduled with John Chen Beckwith. At the workshop on written testimony, held March 5, 1981, Beckwith handed out a two-page guide on structuring statements. Along with his advice to keep testimony simple and use a "natural vocabulary," Beckwith repeatedly stressed that saying how one had felt at the time of the incarceration, and how camp had affected one's life, would be important to the commission's understanding.[16] A report on the March 24 workshop, aimed at those who wished to give oral testimony, gave a more interactive view of participation. In that workshop, the prospective witnesses, before an audience, "were questioned, interrupted, given time limits, and generally went through what might have been an actual hearing" with commissioners; television cameras were set up, and the participants viewed videotaped playbacks during a critique period. "Content, organization, relevancy, body language, voice tone, etc., were commented on by Beckwith. The session was extremely helpful to the audience of about 45 as well as to the participants."[17]

To facilitate easier access for Issei who wanted to testify, Seriguchi also set up meetings with Issei and translators at churches throughout Seattle and at other gathering spots. In addition, translations of the CCRR survey, and information about the commission hearings, were released to *Hokubei Hochi,* the local Japanese-language paper.[18]

In March, CCRR officers also met with their longtime ally Charles Z. Smith, Seattle Chapter JACL board member and professor of law, to receive counsel on preparing for the hearings. Smith advised them that expert testimony about the effects of the internment should be provided by psychiatrists, sociologists, economists, and politicians in addition to the testimony of people who had experienced the effects of E.O. 9066 at first hand. Smith also urged CCRR to observe all commission protocol and courtesies.[19]

All the workshops and meetings were undertaken in preparation for what would be a mock hearing and "remedies workshop" on May 23 at the Nisei Veterans Hall. The idea was to familiarize the community with the overall process of the upcoming hearings and to ensure that the commission received the information it needed to make appropriate recommendations for remedies, or redress. About 200 people, curious and wondering what to expect, turned out on May 23. An air of excitement filled the hall. Smith moderated the program, with introductory remarks made by CWRIC commissioner Hugh Mitchell and Rep. Mike Lowry. Seattle City Attorney Doug Jewett, Washington State Senator Ruthe Ridder, and Ron Mamiya, now a Seattle Municipal Court judge, stood in as "commissioners." Bill Kawata and two other witnesses, Theresa Takayoshi and Bill Iseri, had been selected from previous workshops to testify because their stories were as dramatic as they were filled with sadness, suffering, humiliation, and anger:

> Kawata said he was 11 years old, and he and his father were visiting a business partner in Alaska. One evening the sheriff broke into the house, arrested his father at gun point and jailed him. Kawata was shipped back to Washington and sent to camps where he had to fend for himself. He was not reunited with his father for two years.
>
> "My father had lost 50 pounds when I saw him again," Kawata remembered. After the internment, the two returned to Seattle. "We came back with nothing. My father was a broken man."
>
> Kawata spoke of the loneliness, the humiliation and the terrible fear he felt after such a violent disruption of his life.
>
> "This is a part of my life that's been buried for 39 years," Kawata said. "I wanted to bury it, to forget it. I'm still embarrassed to talk about it."
>
> Kawata said he might not have spoken out if the Japanese American Citizens League committee on redress had not asked him to do so.[20]

Takayoshi told of being a young wife of 24, running an ice-cream parlor with her husband, when the war broke out:

Mrs. Takayoshi, who was half Irish, sought an exemption from going to the camps for herself and her toddler children. The answer came back: She could stay but the two children had to go.

It was no real choice. The whole family went to Minidoka.

A year and a half later, Mrs. Takayoshi applied to be allowed to return to Seattle with her children. The request was denied. She went to Omaha, where the family settled until they finally returned to Seattle in 1967.

They filed a claim under the 1948 claims act for Japanese Americans; they got $100 for their business, which they estimated was worth $10,000 and they had sold for $1,000 in the 10 days they had before being evacuated.[21]

Iseri, a 22-year-old University of Washington student, explained how the Sansei were affected by the imprisonment:

His father never talked about his camp experience, Iseri said. He was a proud, calm, strong man. But then, after being under heavy medication for a serious illness, he began screaming about the misery of camp life, the mistreatment, the unfairness.

After that, Iseri said, he was able, bit by bit, to draw more out of his father. He learned about the loss of his father's dairy and livestock farm, which his grandfather had bought after saving and scrimping for 40 years. In 1973, they went to revisit the Olympic Peninsula spread; as they approached, his father began to cry.[22]

The testimonies were moving, even though it was clear that they had been prepared in advance. The media latched on to the stories, giving the mock hearings much press coverage and the redress movement as a whole a boost of public support.

The second part of the program focused on remedies. Min Yasui, then chair of the JACL National Committee for Redress, explained the national JACL platform for a block-grant fund. Chuck Kato, as past president of the Seattle Chapter JACL, presented the so-called Seattle plan of individual payments. Seriguchi reported the results of the Nikkei survey and outlined other redress proposals.

SEPTEMBER 9–11, 1981: THE CWRIC HEARINGS

By the time the actual commission hearings rolled around, Seattle was prepared. (In fact, some thought Seattle was too prepared.) More than 160 witnesses testified, including a contingent from Portland. Kinoshita thought that as people had heard others testify in the workshops before the hearings, they had said to themselves, "I have a story to tell. I want to tell my story." And, by the time of the actual hearings, there was a huge wave of people willing to talk.

Nevertheless, Kinoshita noted, the Seattle hearings had not been as dramatic as those in some of the other cities. Everything in Seattle had run on time, nobody had demanded more time to speak, and nobody had broken down in the middle of giving testimony. Kinoshita later said she had been concerned that "some of the emotion was lost because it all had been . . . spent with the mock hearing and preparation. . . ." But Kato thought things were better this way: Seattle had made a better impression. Commissioner Bill Marutani seemed to agree. He told Kinoshita that Seattle's hearings were "the best organized."[23]

Also agreeing was Gerald Sato, an attorney from Ventura, California, whose comments about the Seattle Nikkei community were published in Los Angeles, in *Rafu Shimpo*:

> Seattle's Nikkei community is smaller both proportionately and in absolute numbers than Los Angeles Nikkei. Yet, the community leaders in Seattle have been able to keep the redress issue in front of their non-Nikkei neighbors for nearly ten years.
>
> . . . There is not a single Nikkei-oriented newspaper published in the Northwest on a regular basis; yet, the Seattle community leaders have been able to obtain absolutely first rate coverage of the redress campaign in the Northwest from the Seattle and Portland dailies, and from regional newspapers throughout the state. At the hearing, extensive coverage was also provided by the three broadcasting networks, public broadcasting and Dutch television to Europe. All of this has resulted in the matter of redress being a topic of conversation everywhere in the non-Nikkei Seattle community.[24]

Sato had been impressed with the attention to detail at the Seattle hearings, and even with the physical arrangements, which had seemed to help set the tone:

> The commissioners and witnesses sat at two separate tables on the stage of the Seattle Community College auditorium, bathed in the glow of floodlamps against a black curtain backdrop, at angles which allowed everyone

to direct their comments simultaneously to each other, and to the audience. . . . The room itself was air-conditioned, dimly lit, with thick pile car-
peting and softly upholstered chairs—the audience was made to believe that
it was attending a play or concert and behavior followed suit, as coughing
out of turn during a performance would have constituted the grossest breach
of etiquette.[25]

However calm the room may have seemed, and however overprepared
people may have appeared, their stories were still often extremely moving.
June Oyama Takahashi had come down from Alaska to give her painfully honest testimony:

> At the time of Pearl Harbor, I was a student in my second year of high school
> in Petersburg, Alaska. . . . Our family was in the hand laundry business, and
> my father was the local photographer. Exact dates have escaped me, but I
> do remember that it was soon after Pearl Harbor that my father was the
> first man to be picked up by the local authorities and taken to the Petersburg
> jail for reasons unknown to us.
>
> When I used to go home from school, I walked by the jail house, and
> there was a little barred window from which my dad used to call and wave
> to me. I am ashamed now to say that I would take another route home
> because it was too embarrassing for me. I am left with terrible guilt about
> avoiding him.[26]

Emi Somekawa, a retired nurse, described in written testimony how she
and her family had been taken from their home in Portland. Sent first to the
Livestock Exposition Center in North Portland, they were then sent to Tule
Lake, in Northern California, and on to Minidoka. But at the hearings,
Somekawa, departing from her written testimony, instead related her concerns about the medical facilities at Tule Lake and Minidoka, delivering a very
dramatic account:

> It is painful to talk about these happenings and I do not wish to use any
> names, but I am speaking of a professional person who actually observed
> euthanasia performed. A doctor was begged by a family to please adminis-
> ter this patient some kind of medication to put her out of any further mis-
> ery and pain. These situations arose due to many traumatic and psychological
> effects that affected the internees due to the evacuation process.
>
> This was and still is a very sensitive area because it involves Japanese

American doctors and nurses, as well as families who were subjected to euthanasia.

In given circumstances, knowing that euthanasia was and still is considered a crime, taking people out of misery, was the only humane course to take. Had the patient been a member of my family, I would have felt the same way.

The psychological and personal damage caused by the performance of euthanasia is incalculable. The Government by its policy of imprisonment and traumatizing us by not providing adequate medical accommodations to care for all the needs of the patients brought death to many patients.[27]

Stories like these would later cause Miyatake, who also testified at the Seattle hearings, to admit that, in the end, he agreed the commission was an important stage in the redress campaign, if for no other reason, as he would come to say, than that "this exposure of information created a wealth of ideas that were generated by these people. . . . Up until [the hearings], they were ashamed to speak about [imprisonment]." Not only that, Miyatake reasoned, the hearings also provided important history lessons for Japanese Americans who did not even "know their own history." Shosuke Sasaki, in protest of the commission's formation, did not attend the hearings, but he was a subject of discussion between commissioner Bill Marutani and Frank Abe as Abe, giving testimony, tried to express the anti-commission position held by Sasaki and others in Seattle.[28]

The commission continued to gather testimony in nine cities, for a total of twenty days of hearings. Over the next year and a half, it assembled this information, and in December 1982 it published its findings. The CWRIC report meticulously documented the exclusion, removal, and detention of 120,000 people, without benefit of individual review, and their continued exclusion, without regard for their demonstrated loyalty to the United States. It found that "the record does not permit the conclusion that military necessity warranted the exclusion of ethnic Japanese from the West Coast."[29] And, it concluded, if there was no military necessity for the exclusion, then "there was no basis for the detention."[30] The recommendations of the commission were deliberately delayed six months so that any reactions to the idea of monetary compensation would not detract from the findings published in the initial report.[31]

In June 1983 the commission issued its recommendations: (1) that Congress recognize the grave injustice that had been done, and that it offer the nation's apologies for the expulsion and imprisonment of Japanese American citizens; (2) that those convicted of violating the curfew and other laws be pardoned; (3) that Congress direct the executive agencies to which Japanese Americans might apply for the restitution of positions, status, or entitlements lost as a result of acts or events that had taken place during World War II; (4) that Congress establish an educational and humanitarian foundation to address injustices "suffered by an entire ethnic group"; and (5) that Congress appropriate $1.5 billion to pay $20,000 "to each of the approximately 60,000 surviving persons excluded from their places of residence pursuant to Executive Order 9066." The burden would be on the government to locate the survivors, with the oldest survivors to receive payment first. Any remaining funds were to be used for the purposes of public education.[32]

CCRR was elated that the remedies included individual payments in combination with an educational fund; in essence, the commission had followed the major points of the original Seattle plan. The remedies were everything that the supporters of redress had wanted, and now there was a congressional commission to support them. Before the commission had published its findings, however, the Seattle Nikkei community and its supporters had begun work on another form of redress.

6 / Gestures

Early in 1983, a few months before the Commission on Wartime Relocation and Internment of Civilians issued its recommendations, an editorial in the *Seattle Post-Intelligencer* offered the following opinion:

> At the state level, Sen. George Fleming, D-Seattle, has introduced a bill that would serve as an official apology to 38 Japanese Americans who lost their jobs as state employees when they were shipped off to the internment camps. . . . His bill would offer those of the 38 who are still living a token reparation of $5,000. The money is a small gesture that in no way can compensate Americans who lost everything—their property, their businesses, their jobs, their freedom—only because their racial background was Japanese. Still, the gesture should be made.[1]

A "cathartic time": that's what Cherry Kinoshita called the period right after the CWRIC hearings.[2] Another huge step had been taken in the movement for redress. But in late August 1982, while the commission was preparing its report, Kinoshita saw, in articles published by the *Pacific Citizen*, the national publication of the JACL, the news that Priscilla Ouchida, a legislative aide to California assemblyman Patrick Johnston, had led a successful redress campaign at the state level. Assembly Bill 2710, introduced in the California state legislature on February 19, 1982, earmarked $5,000 for state employees who had been fired in 1942. The bill had passed the state assembly on June 7 and the state Senate on August 12, and Governor Jerry Brown had signed it on August 17. As Kinoshita recalled,

I was sitting in the office with Karen Seriguchi and said, "You know, if California can do it, why not Washington? Should we go ahead?" And she said, "Why not?" So then that's where I contacted Ruth Woo, because I knew she had good connections down in Olympia, and then I called Priscilla Ouchida and said, "How did you do it? Give us some help." And . . . we took off on that drive to get the state employees, and that started with Ron Sims and Tim Gojio and Ruth Woo down in Olympia.[3]

Woo was an administrative assistant to Brian Boyle, the commissioner of public lands. She was also a member of a state minority workers' support group, an informal body that met weekly for lunch to exchange ideas about their job experiences and advancement possibilities and about possible legislation affecting minorities in Washington State. Through this network Woo had met Ron Sims, top aide to Sen. George Fleming and leadership coordinator of the Senate Democratic caucus.[4] An African American, and chair of the caucus, Fleming was the only nonwhite member of the Senate. Both Sims and Woo lived in Seattle, and when the state legislature was in session, they often carpooled to Olympia together. It was on one of these drives that Woo raised the issue of redress. As Sims later recalled,

We had gotten into a discussion about Mike Lowry and why Ruth liked Mike, and it was over his work on Japanese reparations, and so between Seattle, where the conversation started, and Olympia, where the conversation ended, . . . we stopped at the Poodle Dog in Tacoma, so it was probably a two-hour discussion, at least. By the time we got down to Olympia, I said, "Why don't we see whether or not we can run a reparations bill in Olympia?"[5]

The Republicans controlled the Senate, and so Sims spoke with Tim Gojio, another member of the informal minority workers' support group and the associate staff counsel for the Senate Republican caucus. "Tim was all in favor of it," Sims recalled, and they began to work on a bill.

Sims asked Frankie Irigon, who worked in the state personnel office, to check the records for information about Japanese Americans who had been working for the state in late 1941 and early 1942.[6] The assignment turned out to be "enormous," according to Sims. Armed with a legislative request to review the records in the state archives, Irigon obtained the records of all the Japanese Americans employed in the State of Washington during those years. The research revealed that the names of 40 Japanese Americans had disappeared from personnel files in the spring of 1942, but the employment records did not show that these employees had been fired. Further research showed that, except for one woman who had gone on "maternity leave," all these employees had resigned, which, at least on paper, implied voluntary departure.[7]

Sims went to the state library and obtained copies of every file it had on Japanese Americans and World War II. He and his staff went through boxes of those files looking for two things: the dates of the specific actions taken by the federal government, and the dates the state was advised of those actions. Then they looked at the employment records of the Japanese Americans during that period, to see when they had left:

> I mean, nobody wanted to be fired. So what people did was, they knew they were gonna go to camp, and so they resigned. That's why we had to show that the resignations were not voluntary. Basically, you saw people not wanting to be terminated. . . . We were able to show the context of the resignation was that it was an involuntary act of resignation, not a voluntary one. . . . When do people get pay raises? Would you ever resign right after a pay raise? The answer is no. Well, several of the people had pay raises, right before they resigned. Or promotions. This was all the stuff you had to look for.[8]

According to Sims, all this detailed work was necessary so that, at the very least, the facts could not be disputed.

At first, no one took this bill seriously: other members of the House and Senate thought this was a "hero" bill, Sims explained, a bill designed to make the legislator look good to a constituent, the kind of bill that enables the lawmaker to "buddy up to the person, but you never are gonna spend a single chit to get it passed. It looks good for public relations, but no big deal. I don't believe in those, and George Fleming, when he ran bills, never ran them to hero. He was gonna run those bills for passes."[9]

The employment records, and the records of federal and state actions with respect to Japanese Americans, were organized into a "nice, huge, thick book"—the book of information that was used to educate the legislators about the 40 state employees who had lost their jobs and about the wartime expulsion. The first person to read this book was Fleming. According to Sims, the information encompassed

> news clips, the state memoranda, and . . . [the] occupation reports. We had the guards . . . at the camps doing notes as to what was going on. So I think

it was seeing all of that just laid out for him so [Fleming] could read at his leisure. He took it home on a Friday night and came back on Monday at work, and I knew the bill was gonna run.[10]

As Sims had begun piecing together the information in his book, others began to realize that he was serious. At the same time, Rep. Art Wang of Tacoma and Rep. Gary Locke of Seattle were introducing their own state-level redress bill in the House. The Democratic and Republican caucuses of the House and Senate also began to take note of Fleming's bill as a real possibility.

Woo, Sims, and Gojio met with Cherry Kinoshita in September and informed her that they could urge Fleming to sponsor the bill. They also informed her that she, JACL, and the Community Committee on Redress/Reparations would have to do the lobbying. "Not knowing then exactly what was involved, I agreed," Kinoshita later recalled, "and that was the beginning of a five-month effort to convince as many state legislators as possible to support the bill." For further advice, she maintained contact with Priscilla Ouchida.

It was at this time that CCRR, having fulfilled its goals on the commission hearings, decided to continue as an organization focused on lobbying for redress legislation. It changed its name to the Washington Coalition on Redress (WCR) to "reflect more accurately the nature and scope of the organization."[11] All 16 of its constituent organizations, with a combined membership of more than 5,000, approved the name change. Kinoshita remained as co-chair, now joined by Chuck Kato (Gordon Hirabayashi had returned to Edmonton).

In November 1982, Democrats regained control of the state House and Senate, and immediately, on November 9, the redress committee of the Seattle Chapter JACL and the Washington Coalition on Redress went to work. Kinoshita wrote a letter, which was signed by all the JACL chapter presidents in Washington and then sent to the 150 state legislators who would be serving the following year. Kinoshita, after explaining that a similar bill had been passed and signed in California, added:

> Legislation will be introduced for approval at the 48th Legislative Session to similarly compensate state employees of Washington for salary losses. Although the federal government has not yet met their moral obligation to redress the wrongs committed against the thousands of loyal Japanese Americans who were imprisoned, in gross violation of their fundamental constitutional rights, our State, like California, can at least compensate for tangible earnings losses.[12]

The November letter produced some responses (from three senators and six representatives) in support of a redress bill, as well as a lot of inquiries from legislators wanting more information about the expulsion and the California bill. As Gojio and Sims laid the groundwork in Olympia, some members of WCR geared up to lobby. Those not interested in direct lobbying concentrated on sustaining the media attention.

While Kinoshita and Seriguchi were thinking up new campaigns, immediately after the hearings, Chuck Kato and other activists were discussing possibilities for a February 19, 1983, Day of Remembrance. Kato thought of doing a "fun run," since jogging was popular at the time. He became chairman of the event. Stan Shikuma, Seriguchi's assistant at the time, suggested a run of 9,066 yards and the printing of T-shirts with the slogan I SURVIVED E.O. 9066, which could be sold to raise funds. The Seattle Chapter JACL board approved the idea and put up some seed money.

"We got permission from the Parks Department to hold the event at Seward Park," Kato recalled:

> I contacted Sam Mitsui, since he was into jogging and ran marathons. He told me what to set up and volunteered to conduct the race timing, determining the winner and all the other details. Because we knew that many couldn't run or walk 9,066 yards, we measured off 9,066 feet and 9,066 inches as well. We wanted everyone to participate. The turnout was fantastic! We ran out of some sizes of T-shirts. People came with their kids and grandkids. It was like a community picnic.[13]

Like the original Day of Remembrance, the event was a successful family outing, drawing out more people, raising funds, and enlightening both Nikkei and non-Nikkei about the World War II expulsion and incarceration.

It had been September 1982 when Woo, Gojio, and Sims informed Kinoshita that they could convince Senator Fleming to sponsor the redress bill. As the new year and legislative session approached, a worried Kinoshita waited for word about Fleming's commitment. She breathed a sigh of relief when WCR learned from Gojio and Sims on January 7, 1983, that Fleming had made the commitment to be the bill's primary sponsor in the Senate.

Kinoshita immediately contacted all the JACL Pacific Northwest District chapter presidents. She also informed them that Reps. Gary Locke and Art Wang would be introducing a similar bill in the House. Kinoshita wrote:

> Let's really get behind this drive! Its success will help toward the national redress effort, and passage of the bill will mean a moral victory even if only a few of the potential claimants ever benefit. Please ask, persuade, and even "twist arms" to have as many individuals as possible write or call the legislators.[14]

When Kinoshita later asked Fleming why he had taken so long to commit himself to being the bill's sponsor, Fleming answered that he had wanted to make sure that "Ron [Sims] and Tim [Gojio] and others had done their homework in gathering their information." He also wanted to ensure that this was a state issue and not a national issue:

> This was something that took place from a state perspective. A state government did this on top of what the federal government had done. And you're asking the state to acknowledge the role that they had played, and you also are asking the state to acknowledge those who were interned. . . . This was a state action, and it was wrong, and it was an opportunity to acknowledge that and to try to undo that—nothing could totally undo it, but it was an admission that, hey, this was wrong, and it shouldn't have happened.[15]

On January 17, Fleming, with Sens. Jack Jones, Jim McDermott, Kent Pullen, and Phil Talmadge as co-sponsors, introduced S.B. 3163. The lobbying, led by Kinoshita, was intense. A statewide letter-writing campaign ensured that the issue was constantly on legislators' minds. Kinoshita made numerous trips to Olympia and organized groups of people to attend hearings and to lobby, testify, and write letters. The grassroots Nikkei support was joined by civil rights organizations and religious and political figures.[16]

Theresa Takayoshi of Seattle wrote to at least a quarter of the legislators, and Denny Yasuhara of Spokane talked to legislators from his district. The conservative bloc from eastern Washington especially needed a reason to vote for the bill. Arguments against redress for state workers ranged from the clever to the absurd: the state should not be responsible for acts resulting from federal executive orders;[17] a $5,000 payment for this violation was an insult;[18] Japan should pay the reparations, since they had started the war.[19] Art Wang even received hate mail telling him, as he said, to go "back to whatever country I supposedly came from."[20]

But Sims had his "book." To those who argued against redress, he would say, "Did you read the book? You *didn't* read the book?" He took offense because he had spent so much time documenting the state's complicity. After all, he said somewhat indignantly, his book of briefing materials was three or four inches thick.[21]

Some politicians went along with the bill because the leadership of both parties supported it. Others had to be convinced, either by contact with constituents or by contact with political and legislative insiders. WCR worked the constituents, and Woo was instrumental in getting support through her informal "minority affairs" group.[22] Others in that group besides Sims, Gojio, and Irigon were also working their connections. As Fleming's bill gained steam, Naomi Iwata-Sanchez, in Gov. John Spellman's office, helped gain the governor's interest. Joan Yoshitomi and Grayce Chin were on Senator Jim McDermott's office staff.[23]

Woo also knew a lot of people in Olympia. In one of the Friday meetings of the informal group, Sims mentioned that Eugene Prince of Walla Walla needed a reason to vote for the bill: "To Gene, it was, 'Why would I do this?' and Ruth got on the phone and called Gene up and said, 'We need your support, and this is why.' And all of sudden we had Gene because he, I think, had a huge regard [for Ruth]."[24]

Senate Substitute Bill 3163 was introduced by Fleming on February 3, 1983, restricting the eligibility of heirs to spouses only. Fleming's words boomed from the Senate floor: "I am frightened, as you should be, that if we do not learn from our mistakes, we will repeat them."[25] The bill passed the Senate with only 11 dissenting votes.

In the House there was a tougher battle. Locke and Wang argued passionately for their bill, with Locke's speech seeming to address those who might vote against redress because of the wartime wrongs committed by the Japanese government:

Let me point out one thing to be very clear. I am of Chinese descent. My mother was born and raised in China, in Hong Kong. And during World War II, Hong Kong was occupied by Japanese forces, and many of our rel-

atives died in World War II or in the war in China. My mom has not forgotten the war, and she does not particularly like the Japanese. She is still
fighting the war. As are many Japanese individuals still fighting the war, particularly with respect to Chinese. However, she does not understand how
this country, to which she [immigrated] and of which she is now an
American citizen, could have unilaterally, totally, and unconstitutionally
deprived a hundred and twenty thousand American citizens of their rights,
without due process, without trial, without any accusation or any type of
fair hearing. We are a country of laws and a constitution, and however small
this measure may be, either we stand for our principles, or we do not. Either
we take the opportunity that is given to us to redress these wrongs, or we
say that these constitutional rights are convenient only when we desire
them.[26]

The House passed the bill, 57 to 37, on May 6, 1983.[27] A week later, Gov.
Spellman signed it. All 40 employees who had "voluntarily" resigned received
payments. Two of the 40 were deceased, including Captain George Sawada,
a medic who had died in action during World War II, and payments were
made to their widows.

Many believed that the bill's passage was a testament to the rightness and
timeliness of the bill and to the dogged persistence of WCR and its team of
contacts in the halls of Olympia and throughout the state. The organizing
capabilities of both WCR and the informal support group had brought
together a well-informed, responsive team of politicians and grassroots lobbyists from JACL and the Japanese / Asian American communities. WCR was
also responsible for procuring overwhelming support for the bill from other
civil and human rights organizations and from church groups, political figures,
and the media.[28] As Sims later said, the bill

became an issue of the state, itself finding a way to arrive at a peace with its
own decisions. Some people were not there to collect. They had passed away.
But what I think we saw was a process, in one session—this was a single-
session bill, which is unheard of; to have something that's not even on the
radar screen come in and all of a sudden develop a momentum and a life
of its own was pretty extraordinary to see . . . where you could say, the state
had complicity. We were not at arm's length. We embraced the decision by
the army to take our workers, terminate their employment, and we did not

stand up against the federal government when people were removed from their homes and put in camps.

So I think you saw a legislature willing to say, hey, let's cleanse our souls somewhat, put that decision behind us. And this is legislation that took. It became a real good moral issue, and that's how it moved the debate on the floor.[29]

The successful campaign by WCR and the informal support group had also caught the attention of the Commission on Wartime Relocation and Internment of Civilians, which cited the payments to Washington State workers, and to former employees of California, Los Angeles, and San Francisco, as a precedent for "remedial measures."[30]

One could also argue that the Washington community had clout. Whether it was the friendly politicians, their aides, or just the rightness of the bill, the lobbying efforts succeeded. Politicians, being politicians, must have felt it was politically safe to support the legislation.

The measure's quick passage also demonstrated that an organized opposition was nowhere in sight. The measure had encountered little antagonism; by and large, the few non-Nikkei arguments against redress were not taken seriously. But even with the high turnout for the CWRIC hearings, there was still some resistance in the Nikkei community itself. Some believed that redress would mean reliving the pain of incarceration, and there was a strong belief in the potential for backlash, but each success both educated the public and enabled more Japanese Americans to testify.

At the state level, Frank Kinomoto and Miye Ishihara, who had both worked for the State Tax Commission, spoke about their experiences before the state legislature. Ishihara testified, "I was called to the office of the chairman of the Tax Commission, and he said to me that I would be dismissed at the end of February 1942, solely because of my ancestry."[31] Although many found their feelings difficult to express, they set the record straight. Their statements that these things had happened, and that the forced evacuation and internment were real, made it possible for redress to pass and enabled a community to find its voice.

Later, in the redress campaigns for fired Seattle School District and municipal employees, and for people incarcerated during the war, the WCR network and its contacts would be used again and again. In the interim, however, backlash against a memorial sculpture proposed for Camp Harmony, at the

Puyallup Fairgrounds, provided another chance to gain media attention for redress.

MEMORIAL OF CAMP HARMONY

It turned out to receive more publicity and attention than anything
I have ever done. Not because this is great or anything like that. It just
happened to be at the right moment. That's life.
—George Tsutakawa, at the unveiling of his sculpture *Harmony*[32]

In early 1981, while the Community Committee on Redress / Reparations was preparing for the CWRIC hearings, Emi Somekawa of the Puyallup Chapter JACL had been talking to Rep. Dan Grimm of her state district about the possibility of having some type of memorial placed at the Puyallup Fairgrounds. Many participants in the 1978 Day of Remembrance caravan to Puyallup had been so moved by the emotion of the day that they felt a permanent commemoration at the site of the World War II imprisonment would be appropriate.

Grimm was receptive to the idea, and, with Rep. George Walk, also of Puyallup, introduced a bill in the state House, asking the state to appropriate $30,000 for a memorial sculpture to be designed and fabricated by the internationally renowned sculptor George Tsutakawa. In presenting the bill in the House, Grimm remarked, "Instead of trying to forget about [the internment], maybe it's better we remember so it may never happen again." Sen. Marc Gaspard sponsored the bill in the state Senate, along with Sens. George Fleming, Ted Haley, Jerry Hughes, and Ruthe Ridder.

The legislature authorized $26,000 for the memorial. The Western Washington Fair Association Board approved the site and design, and it allocated funds from its budget. Everything seemed to be moving smoothly.

In May 1982, however, the Puyallup chapter of the American Legion objected to the memorial, proposing instead a Pearl Harbor memorial. Vern Hill, operator of a funeral home in Puyallup, had initiated the Pearl Harbor proposal, stating that Japanese Americans had entered the camps voluntarily, that some groups had sent radio transmissions from inside the camps, and that Japanese Americans had entered the camps for their own safety. The Puyallup chapter carried its proposal to the state convention of the American Legion, which adopted a resolution opposing any memorial of the internment. The American Legion was unable to cancel the project entirely, but in early 1983 the organization did convince the Western Washington Fair Association Board to change the site of the memorial: instead of being inside the fairgrounds, it was to be placed in the parking lot across the street from the entrance gate.

This action outraged both the Japanese American community and Tsutakawa, the sculptor, who decided to back out of the project, and it brought national media attention to the board. As Tsutakawa related, "I didn't want it to be stuck in a parking lot, vulnerable to an act of vandalism. So I just said, 'In that case, I won't do it.'"[33] Henry Miyatake, hearing of the planned changes, was also wary of possible vandalism to the proposed sculpture. He and Tsutakawa had reason to be concerned: vandals had bombed monuments at Manzanar and Tule Lake, both in remote desert areas, and used them for target practice. Miyatake and Tsutakawa both also knew that more attention would be paid to the memorial if it were on the fairgrounds proper.

Miyatake approached Roger Shimizu, an attorney and an officer of the Asian Lawyers Association in Washington State, about the possibility of suing the American Legion on grounds of defamation, or on other grounds, because of false statements made by Vern Hill and, perhaps, the board's breach of contract. Shimizu agreed to attend a March 7, 1983, meeting with the board, with Somekawa, Miyatake, Ben Nakagawa, Chuck Kato, and Tom Shigio also in attendance. Shimizu recalled:

> After some discussion and a direct threat of a lawsuit, the Fair Board convened an emergency meeting and reversed their decision and agreed that the monument should be sited inside the Fairgrounds and not in the parking lot. Ben and Chuck, especially Ben, wanted me to indicate that I was authorized to sue and to say as much in the meeting. I recall so doing. I recall the members of the Fair Board and staff indicating that a lawsuit was not necessary.[34]

By this time, the board's actions had been noted across the nation, in various newspapers. As in previous controversies related to the World War II expulsion and incarceration, more media attention and scrutiny allowed the issue of the sculpture's placement to become another educational tool for redress activists. In this case, the issue became an educational opportunity for the Puyallup Monument Committee of the Seattle Chapter JACL.[35]

Vern Hill was not the only person who made outrageous comments, and

Shimizu and others responded to numerous letters that had been published in Puyallup-area newspapers. As Shimizu said, "Once again, the protestors had linked Japanese Americans with the actions and activities of the Japanese Imperial Army and Navy during the war. I recall several positive editorials in various newspapers in this area as well, however. Overall, the fair board's actions raised public awareness and interest in the monument project." In addition, according to Shimizu, because people were so outraged by the stance of the American Legion and the waffling of the Western Washington Fair Association Board, many who before had stayed on the sidelines now became strong redress activists. The publicity and controversy were helpful in fundraising, too: in a little over two months, the monument committee raised $13,000.[36] This response surprised the committee, and a second donor plaque had to be ordered because the space for donor names on the original had filled up.

Commissioned in 1981, the memorial had its appropriation cut to about $13,000 by the 1983 legislature, or less than half of what had originally been proposed. Nevertheless, with the Western Washington Fair Association, the Puyallup Chapter JACL, and the Seattle Chapter JACL committed to $5,000 each as seed money, and with Gov. John Spellman committing another $13,700 from the governor's contingency fund, the project's funding remained sound.

Much of the donated money was used to ensure a large gathering at the dedication and unveiling ceremony, held on August 21, 1983. Gov. Spellman, who earlier in the year had demonstrated his firm support of redress for state workers wrongfully terminated in 1942, agreed to speak at the ceremonies. According to Shimizu, this was a major accomplishment, since neither the Washington Historical Society (which had designated the site as a state historical area) nor the Western Washington Fair Association Board had indicated that a ceremony was planned or even desired. As at the 1978 Day of Remembrance, attendees at the August 21 ceremony were registered according to their camp blocks and given name tags to wear during the day. Between 700 and 800 participants remembered their four months in captivity at the fairgrounds, 41 years before. They watched the unveiling of the memorial, which was dedicated to future generations, and heard Spellman reiterate their own thoughts about the imprisonment:

> I've received letters asking if I had forgotten Pearl Harbor, if I had forgotten the mothers of those who gave their lives in defense of this country. I haven't forgotten. But all those letters reflect a common confusion: con-

fusing war between Japan and the United States with the mass deprivation of [citizens'] constitutional rights solely because of their race. Their freedom was trampled on for no good reason.[37]

Once again, redress activists had taken a potentially harmful attack, answered it, and turned it into a positive educational and media opportunity.

"NO MORE, NO LESS": THE CITY OF SEATTLE

After a difficult time finding a job in the pre-war years, I was finally employed by City Light in October 1941 as a clerk with a salary which provided a relatively comfortable living for me.

I had come from the small town of Skykomish to Seattle, completed business school very rapidly, found friends at the Japanese Methodist Church, and was the happiest I had been in my life. Then Pearl Harbor! Fathers of some of my friends were taken to internment camps, a curfew was imposed on anyone of Japanese ancestry, and within several months we were informed that we were laid off from our positions because of the "National Crisis."

—Sumiko Kuriyama[38]

One of the major components of the lobbying effort on behalf of the state workers had been garnering the support of public officials. Mayor Charles Royer of Seattle, who had expressed his support for redress during the 1978 Day of Remembrance, also supported the move in the legislature, as did Seattle City Council member Dolores Sibonga.

During communications with Sibonga about the state bill, Cherry Kinoshita had asked about the possibility of introducing a similar measure for Seattle city workers who had been terminated. Sibonga said yes, and she sent a memorandum to Susan B. Pavlou, Seattle's director of personnel, requesting information on the termination of city employees of Japanese ancestry between 1942 and 1947.[39] Sibonga received the following report from Pavlou:

A search of the personnel and payroll records has revealed five employees of Japanese ancestry who appear to have been terminated from City employment as a direct result of the Federal Executive Order 9066 of 1942. . . .

The 1942–43 Annual Report of the Civil Service Department includes the following paragraph: "When it became necessary, because of military reasons, to evacuate Japanese from this area, we provided for the separation of any of them who were working for the City, and we took action withholding the names of any who were on our registers from certification for appointment."

This statement, supported by the records of that period, indicates that upon separation of these employees in March 1942, no Japanese were certified and therefore no Japanese were regularly hired by the City for the duration of the war. The payroll register for April 1942, for example, shows no employees with Japanese surnames. Furthermore, it was not until late 1945 and early 1946 that the City began regularly appointing those persons of Japanese ancestry.[40]

Attached to the memo were the files of five employees—three junior clerks and two intermediate clerks—whose salaries ranged from $115 to $140 per month and who were all terminated on March 20, 1942. Also attached was a letter from the superintendent of the City of Seattle Department of Lighting to the Civil Service Commission, requesting permission to "lay off, out of order," the five employees "due to the present National crisis, and taking into consideration the best interest of the persons concerned and the Department."

In the ensuing months, Royer worked with Sibonga on determining the appropriate actions the city could take to remedy the injustices of the wartime incarceration. While Sibonga developed a city ordinance granting reparations to city workers, Royer worked on a resolution urging the Washington State congressional delegation, the U.S. Conference of Mayors, and the National League of Cities to support the adoption of the CWRIC recommendations.[41]

In January 1984, Alan Osaki, Sibonga's legislative assistant, sent WCR a draft of a redress ordinance along with a proposed timetable for its passage. Kinoshita, in order to devote more of her time to lobbying for the national redress bill, gave Tim Otani, recently hired as regional director of the JACL Pacific Northwest District, responsibility for organizing on behalf of the City of Seattle ordinance. Otani and his aide, Stan Shikuma, picked up where Kinoshita left off, contacting people and lining up speakers for the hearings that were scheduled for February 15. Fifteen speakers agreed to testify, including Mike Lowry, Charles Z. Smith (now a state Supreme Court justice), and representatives from the Democratic Party Central Committee, the Washington State Commission on Asian American Affairs, and the American

Friends Service Committee. Also testifying would be Thomas Kobayashi and Sumiko Haji Kuriyama, two of the Seattle City Light clerks who had lost their jobs. Like the hearings before the CWRIC and the state legislature, the city hearings provided another outlet for information about the long-term effects of the racism that had been directed toward those of Japanese ancestry. As Kuriyama testified,

> It is difficult to admit, but at that time I felt shame and embarrassment, rather than anger—shame that I was of Japanese ancestry. How simple life would have been if I were a Caucasian like so many of my friends. My parents had taught me that I was an American, that the United States was my home chosen by them, and that I must be a loyal citizen. My youthful naiveté and idealism of those days is difficult to fathom now. However, thanks to this idealism, I had the faith and hope which brought me through trying days, months, and years.
>
> With the passage of years, with varied experiences, and with age, I look back with shame *as an American* that we allowed civil liberties to be taken away from more than 120,000 individuals of Japanese ancestry.
>
> Unlike the protagonist in Orwell's *1984* who had vague recollections of some events in the past, but who could find no record of those events nor of some of the people involved, let us insure that the pages of the history of the United States do not leave out, alter, or fabricate any events of those days. The history books must record the facts as they occurred—no more, no less.[42]

Ordinance 111571, introduced by Sibonga, stated that "in the interest of fairness, justice and honor, The City of Seattle should make reparation to City employees of Japanese ancestry who were terminated, laid-off or dismissed from City employment pursuant to Executive Order No. 9066" and called for payments of $5,000 to each former employee.[43] On March 1, 1984, the Seattle City Council's finance committee, chaired by Sibonga, passed the ordinance. The council passed the bill without dissent on March 5, and Mayor Royer signed it the following day.[44] What was surprising was the ease with which it passed; as Tim Otani said later, "It sailed through. There was little opposition. And the numbers were small, so what was there to object to?"

But what if the numbers had been greater? And what if there had been organized opposition? WCR and other redress activists were soon to find out.

TO DO THE RIGHT THING: THE SEATTLE SCHOOL DISTRICT

After reading the articles that were printed in the newspapers which led to our resignation, I became very very angry to think that the Seattle School District did not show the strength to back us up in any manner. If we were found or felt to be other than loyal American citizens, we would not have been hired in the first place. I see now that we were pressured to resign without a proper hearing and this was an infringement of our rights as citizens of this country.

—May Daty Namba[45]

We want to assure them all that we really feel this is best, at least for the duration. When we started this thing, it was not from any grudge against the American Japanese, but only for the safety of our children. I really feel that they've done the right thing.

—Esther M. Sekor[46]

The state and city redress efforts looked promising, and so the Washington Coalition on Redress began to turn a portion of its attention to the Seattle School District. The story of the former school employees presented an interesting challenge, on two fronts. First, although the state and city redress efforts had paralleled efforts in California, a challenge to a school district would break new ground and further the national redress movement. Second, the events that had led to the forced resignation of 27 school clerks in early 1942 were fascinating. As early as the fall of 1982, Cherry Kinoshita had been wondering what the real story was behind this "mass resignation."[47]

Behind the many headlines of the early 1940s were painful but little-known stories. WCR had first learned of the former school district clerks from a single news article, complete with picture, titled "Japanese Girls Resign Positions in City Schools," which had been found in a collection of news clippings gathered by Yoriko Watanabe Sasaki, Shosuke Sasaki's wife.[48] This story interested Kinoshita and Mako Nakagawa, then president of the Seattle Chapter JACL. Making an effort to locate all 27 of these employees, Kinoshita—who knew several of "the girls" referred to in the story—learned that 10 were still living in the Seattle area, 15 were residing out of state, and 2 were deceased.[49] Intrigued by the possibility of redress, she wondered if the women would entertain the idea of seeking compensation from the Seattle Public Schools.

To make sure there were no legal deterrents to such an effort, Kinoshita checked with Michael Hoge, Seattle School District legal counsel, who, to her surprise, was immediately supportive. He advised that an appropriate resolution would have to be introduced to the seven-member school board by a board member. Nakagawa asked her friend T. J. Vassar, vice president of the school board, to introduce the resolution. With that hurdle cleared in the early summer of 1983, Kinoshita and Nakagawa called a meeting of the 10 former clerks who still lived in the Seattle area, and most of them attended the meeting.

The purpose of the meeting, Kinoshita told them, was to determine whether these former employees of the Seattle Public Schools had been wrongfully dismissed in 1942, and, if so, to determine whether they wished to pursue redress from the school district. Nakagawa, an elementary school principal with the Seattle School District, added that the school district had been supportive of her as an individual; she passionately encouraged these women to pursue action against the district and seek redress for their dismissals. The pro-redress mood in the state and the makeup of the school board gave Nakagawa confidence that redress was winnable. She urged the women to tell their stories; only through sharing their experiences and exposing the injustice of the past could similar injustices be prevented, she said. When Nakagawa finally sat down, the room was silent.

After some time to let Nakagawa's words settle, Kinoshita asked each woman to recount her experience. Slowly, the women began relating the dry facts, but it did not take long before each of them was struggling to contain her feelings.

One woman told her story as if it had happened the day before. Called into the office of the assistant superintendent, she had been told that her employment, along with that of the other clerks of Japanese ancestry, was a detriment to the school district. She was also told that she was expected to attend a meeting the following day, where she should strongly urge her Japanese American peers to resign from their respective posts. The assistant superintendent warned that each of the "girls" would be fired if they did not resign. This woman vividly recounted her attempts to compose herself in the ladies' room after the confrontation, so that she could take public transportation home.

Another recalled her dismay at being asked to sign the letter of mass resignation. She had been proud to be helping her family with the money from her job. Her father had recently been arrested by the FBI; she saw herself as the primary breadwinner. She had known of the fuss being made in the papers about Japanese American clerks, but somehow she did not think it was relevant to herself. She shared how deeply her feelings burned and how, at the same time, she had felt at a total loss, with no target on which to vent her anger.

Yet another said she had felt perplexed. Unable to express her discomfort about signing her name to the resignation letter, she had reluctantly agreed but had still been troubled and had gone so far as to stop at a public phone booth on her way home to ask that her name be struck from the letter. She was told it was too late: the letter had already been posted. "How is it," she asked, "that I could feel like a culprit and yet know I did nothing wrong?"

These stories astounded Nakagawa. To her, the issue had simply been a matter of rectifying a past wrong. She had been aware of the facts, but she had not been attuned to the emotions of the people whom those facts had dramatically affected. Nakagawa was embarrassed by her call for speakers and humbled by the emotional power of the stories: these 40-year-old wounds were still fresh.

When the group eventually came around to discussing the options, Kinoshita explained the process of obtaining redress. Vassar was willing to propose a resolution to the Seattle School Board, calling for monetary redress for all the former employees. For the resolution to be effective, as many women as possible needed to make presentations about their experiences. Like many other Nikkei who had been asked to testify before the commission or the state legislature, the group initially balked at the thought of making public statements. One woman sharply retorted, "It was not us that made the mistake that caused pain to so many. Why is it up to us to go through the ordeal of having to make public statements?" Another stated, "I don't trust what I might do if I'm forced to expose my private pain." Still another said, "They should apologize and make proper restitution. Why should we do anything?" Another asked if there was any other way.

In the middle of the emotionally charged exchange, May Daty Namba became one of the first to venture her consent to making a statement to the board, but with the proviso that she would not be the only one. Namba, with no background in public speaking, later admitted that she had been concerned about the possible reactions of the women around her. She had also felt petrified at presenting her story to the board. Namba decided to speak up because she was still very angry. She also said that Nakagawa's challenge to the women to tell their stories, and Kinoshita's obvious commitment, were huge influences. After Namba volunteered, a number of other women agreed to take the first step and at least write out statements for the board. Step two of the Seattle School District redress effort then got under way.

T. J. Vassar called Mako Nakagawa in a fit of excitement.

"You won't believe this! I just happened to ask the district archivist to see if she could find any news articles on the dismissal of the Japanese American women you're working with. I thought she would find the article we already have, but I sure didn't expect what I got. You just wait there, because I have something to show you!"

Vassar had grown up on Beacon Hill, a Seattle neighborhood where many Japanese Americans had lived, and he still lived there. He was aware of the state and city redress movements. When Nakagawa had first shown Vassar the reprint of the article on the former school clerks, he already knew that both May Sasaki (then Seattle Chapter JACL president-elect) and Nakagawa had been incarcerated as children in animal stalls at the Puyallup Fairgrounds. "But like a lot of us," he would later say, "I didn't hear about that in school. I didn't know anything about it growing up. So here was a situation that came to me and I thought, here's an opportunity to do something"—an opportunity, he said, that eventually turned into one of his proudest achievements as an educator.[50]

When Vassar arrived at Nakagawa's office, he was holding a large packet, straight from the district archives, containing news clippings and documents, all concerning the Japanese American clerks.

The campaign to fire them had been initiated in late February 1942 by a Gatewood Elementary School parent and her committee, who received prominent coverage in all the local papers. One headline read SCHOOL MOTHERS PROTEST JAPANESE OFFICE GIRLS: GATEWOOD GROUP OPENS CAMPAIGN TO HAVE NIPPONESE DISMISSED. Large pictures showed these mothers staging a demonstration and proudly circulating petitions seeking the dismissal of all "Japanese office girls." The parent, Esther M. Sekor, is quoted as saying, "We always had a white girl until last Fall and we resent this change particularly because we have no Japanese students in our school. This is a white district."[51] In the newspaper clippings, as well as in the school documents, the words and phrases used to describe the clerks were "Japanese," "American-born Japanese clerk," and, even worse, "Jap girls."[52]

Reading these news clippings and documents was almost as stunning to Nakagawa as listening to the former clerks tell their own stories. She remembered Namba asking, "Where were the people from the schools who were supposed to stand up for us? We worked hard. We were loyal Americans. Didn't that count for something?"

But a few voices had spoken up for these young Americans. Several principals timidly attested to the good work of the young women. Some letters to the editor in Vassar's packet of clippings reminded readers that the clerks were Americans by birthright and education. They warned against judging people solely on ancestry: "To repay their years of faithful living up to American ideals by Nazi-like discrimination against the whole race seems very inconsistent with the beliefs we profess," one person wrote.[53] But these voices were drowned out by the growing alarmist publicity. More letters read like the following:

> The mere fact that a child is born in this country should not give him the rights and privileges of citizenship. The fourteenth amendment, granting automatic citizenship to American born, was placed there for the protection of the Negro and at that time the great infiltration of Japs were not even thought of.[54]

With public pressure mounting, Worth McClure, Seattle School District superintendent, wrote a memorandum filled with contradictions to the school board on February 20. Although he closed his memo with a strong warning that "nothing is more divisive of national unity and teamwork than a series of unreasoning witch-hunts," McClure also assured the board that the FBI had "been provided with a complete list" of names and addresses of the clerks and their families. The superintendent also added that he had asked the federal agency to notify him if there were any doubts as to the "loyalty of any girl on the list." Right after he submitted his memo to the board, McClure, oddly, left town on "district business," according to the historian Louis Fiset,[55] and the situation with the clerks was left to the assistant superintendent, Samuel A. Fleming.

Concerned about the growing pressure from the Gatewood mothers and other district constituents, Fleming called one of his former students, James "Jimmy" Sakamoto, with whom he had kept in touch over the years. Sakamoto, editor of the *Japanese American Courier*, a community newspaper, and a founding member of JACL, was a well-known community leader. He later told his wife that Fleming had asked him to approach the clerks about resigning.[56]

On February 24, 1942, Sakamoto called a meeting of all the clerks, to be held at the *Courier* office. All 27 of the young women attended. May Ota Higa, a former clerk who now resided in California, later wrote to Kinoshita about that meeting:

> Mr. Sakamoto pleaded with us and told us that the honorable thing for us to do was to resign for the following reasons:
>
> 1. As loyal American citizens, we should cooperate with those in leadership.
> 2. As good American citizens of Japanese heritage, this action is in keeping with the tradition and teaching of our culture. We must "gracefully" resign.
> 3. If we were fired, there would be a bad record for us and, not only would that be a disgrace for Nisei in general, but would also pose difficulty later when we seek employment. *He did indicate that we would be fired if we did not resign.*[57]

Several women later described Sakamoto as having been extremely tense. They recalled his impassioned plea: "If I could give my arm to save these jobs, I would gladly do so." Arguing that their resignation would prove their loyalty to America, he read a prepared letter of mass resignation to the young women and pleaded for their signatures. His personal dynamism and emotional appeal persuaded the young women, and each of them affixed her name to the following letter:

> TO THE SCHOOL BOARD:
>
> We, the undersigned American citizens of Japanese ancestry, have learned that our presence as employes in the Seattle School system has been protested by certain persons and organizations.
>
> Most of us have received our education in the local schools, and have been proud of the fact, as we have been proud of our positions as employes.
>
> We do not take this action in any spirit of defeat, but believe we can by our resignations demonstrate beyond dispute that we have the best interest of the school system at heart. We take this step to prove our loyalty to the school system and the United States by not becoming a contributing factor to dissension and disunity when national unity in spirit

and deed is vitally necessary to the defense of and complete victory for America.

We bear no ill will toward those who have protested our employment in the school system. We feel that is their privilege.

We only hope that the welfare of the schools will be served by our action in resigning the positions we now occupy.

Finally, we wish to express our heartfelt appreciation to the School Board, the superintendents, the principals, and teachers for the kind treatment accorded us.

Signed this twenty-fourth day of February, 1942.

Martha T. Inouye	Kiku Tomita	May Ota
Esther K. Uchimura	Chizuko Ikeda	Emi Kamachi
Kyoko Kikuchi	Marjorie Ota	Masa Yamamura
Mariko Ozaki	Ruby Shitama	Anna Yamada
May Daty	Toyo Okuda	Ayako Morita
Kay K. Yokoyama	Alice M. Kawanishi	Kazuko Kuroda
Yoshiko Kozu	Sally Shimanaka	Jane Sugawara
Ai Takizawa	Mitsuko Murao	Yuri Ike
Yoshiko Yano	Teruko Nakata	Ayame Ike[58]

As far as the school district was concerned, a possible disaster had been circumvented. The Gatewood mothers were threatening to campaign against the pending Seattle School District levy. Fleming must have felt relieved, but, even with the letter of mass resignation in hand, the assistant superintendent could not accept the resignation without the school board's approval. From February 25 to February 27, the day the board was to take official action, the Seattle papers were filled with stories of the resignations. That day, several citizens spoke out against the board's having accepted the resignations. A petition was also submitted, with signatures from more than a thousand University of Washington students, calling the Gatewood petition "undemocratic, intolerant, disrespectful of the rights of American citizens."[59]

After meeting in closed session for more than an hour, the school board emerged, only to praise "the girls" for their hard work and loyalty and thank them for their contribution to the Seattle schools. The board also commended the clerks for the graceful action of their "voluntary" resignations, which the board had decided, after lengthy discussion, to accept.

After the decision was announced, Sekor was quoted as saying, "I think that's very white of those girls. They have our appreciation and thanks."[60]

Vassar, Nakagawa, Kinoshita, May Sasaki, and May Namba pored over the old articles. Learning the details of the past brought more energy and determination to the group. Vassar's resolution was to be presented to the board on April 11, 1984, with the vote scheduled for two weeks later. Meanwhile, as active members of JACL and other community organizations, Sasaki, Nakagawa and Kinoshita used their contacts to seek letters of support for the former clerks, and all three of them were surprised at how eager people were to help out. Several individuals called and volunteered to circulate petitions. In a short time, letters were pouring in from such organizations as the American Friends Service Committee, El Centro de la Raza, the Church Council of Greater Seattle, and the Women's International League for Peace and Freedom.[61] Later, the district also received letters of opposition to the school redress effort, but this time, unlike in 1942, letters favoring the resolution far out numbered those in opposition.

Kinoshita had scheduled Mayor Royer and state Sen. George Fleming to lead off the presentations. On the appointed day, these officials stated their support for T. J. Vassar's Resolution 1984–8 and launched the testimonies of the former clerks.

The Seattle School District boardroom was filled with interested citizens, the press and broadcast media, district personnel, and many relatives and friends from the Japanese American community. Their murmurs hushed as the first of the former school clerks approached the microphone.

May Daty Namba's calm articulation was in direct contrast to the painful words of her testimony, setting a refined tone for all who followed. "At a young age," she stated, "I bore the brunt of the fear and hatred of a few concerned mothers. There was no way I was going to be disloyal to my country."[62]

The second presenter, Alice M. Kawanishi, pointed out the irony of what had happened. "Looking back," she told the room, "I believe the maneuvered resignation was not necessary; evacuation was mandated by an Executive Order. We were taken to Puyallup fairgrounds." In addition, Kawanishi pointed out, "the very school system which taught us about democracy, liberty, and justice for all, failed to support and defend the Americans of Japanese ancestry against the mass deprivation of rights of citizens." As if responding to Kawanishi's comments, Toyo Okuda Cary, the woman who had been called into the office of the assistant superintendent, recounted her story of being told by the highest school district official that she must resign.

Becky Sasaki, May Sasaki's teenage daughter, was the final presenter at the first meeting. Becky made her presentation with the sense of urgency typical of youth, speaking first about the glossing over of Executive Order 9066 in high school textbooks. She related her fear that her peers would not understand the past, given the cursory view of history that was being presented: if they failed to learn just how unjust and racist the camps were, then there was no assurance that history would not someday repeat itself. In her final words to the school board, she stated, "The school board of the past allowed the fear and racism of a community to cloud its judgment. It's time for the school board *now* to correct that error: to act as a role model for its students, for the sake of the victims, and as a stand for *justice.*"

On April 25, when the board was to take its vote, the room was filled beyond capacity. Publicity had drawn even more citizens, reporters, and TV cameras, charging the atmosphere. As if seeking to answer questions lingering in the public's mind, the testimony at this meeting focused on why, in 1942, the young clerks had resigned if they really had not wanted to leave their jobs. Jane Sugawara Okada pointed out that children of the 1930s and 1940s were "raised to be obedient . . . and not make waves." Ai Takizawa Koshi said they "were coerced into signing the resignation letter" by being "told we would be doing our part for the war effort." Koshi continued, "We were young, immature, and bewildered and thought that there was no other alternative." Sally Shimanaka Kazama agreed: "Most of us very reluctantly signed, though there were many unanswered questions. There were no other options: resign or be fired."

But the publicity from the first meeting had also brought out opponents, who may have been aligned with Americans for Historical Accuracy.[63] Their literature and testimony suggested that the internment camps had never existed at all or were pleasant, safe sanctuaries in which to wait out the war. After using their allotted time, they disrupted the meeting with heckling and other outbursts, and several tried to address the board a second and third time. The board president rapped the gavel several times to regain control of the meeting. Every Japanese American in the audience remained grimly silent.

Resolution 1984–8 passed by a narrow margin: there were 4 votes in favor and 2 against, with 1 abstention. Nakagawa was disappointed by the closeness of the vote but happy that the resolution had passed. As the decision was announced, a man sitting next to Nakagawa shouted across the room, "We should've lynched them in Puyallup while we had the chance!"

A recess was called, and most of the audience filed out of the auditorium. Some, oblivious to what had been shouted, were excitedly talking about the vote, but Peter Koshi, brother-in-law of one of the former clerks, was shouting at the man who had been sitting next to Nakagawa: "We, too, fought for our country and have rights as American citizens." At the same time, the man shouted something to the effect that if Koshi didn't like it here, he should "go back to Japan." As the all too common argument ensued, the redress activists congratulated themselves and the former clerks. One of them had slipped out to another part of the building: Mako Nakagawa found May Namba in the personnel office, submitting her application for re-employment.

Mike Hoge, legal counsel for the Seattle School District, said that he would have liked to see the women receive their redress money as soon as possible, but it was his opinion that this kind of monetary distribution would fall under the "gift" category and therefore would not be allowable. The money was to be placed in escrow until Ken Eikenberry, the state attorney general, could determine the method of legal disbursement.

Cherry Kinoshita responded to this ruling by meeting with anyone who would meet with her on the issue. She sent out letter after letter, trying to get a favorable resolution. She even quietly urged people to campaign for Eikenberry's opponent in the fall election, in the hope that he would be more inclined to support redress for the former clerks. But Eikenberry was hesitant, even after garnering the support of highly influential people, including officials from the Office of the Superintendent of Public Instruction, Sens. Fleming and Talmadge, and Reps. Locke, Jesse Wineberry, and Janice Niemi (who all had written to him and urged prompt action). Finally, on August 9, 1985, after a series of written skirmishes, Kinoshita finally received a letter from James K. Pharris, senior assistant attorney general:

> As a matter of law, further legislation would be required before the Seattle School District could recognize a "moral obligation" as a basis for making reparation payments. We continue to encourage the passage of such an act as a prerequisite to the making of reparation payments.[64]

The quicker option of a decision from the state attorney general was now out of reach. Kinoshita would have to take her case to a system with which she had become more than familiar: the state legislature.

Gary Locke and Art Wang again gave their support and introduced H.B. 1415 on January 14, 1986.[65] Once again, the time had come to lobby. This time, young Sansei like Becky Sasaki and Jerry Shigaki, Seattle JACL chapter president-elect, shouldered many of the lobbying tasks, making several trips to

Olympia to lobby on behalf of the former school clerks. Victory was claimed on February 15, when the bill passed the state House of Representatives by a vote of 82 to 15.[66] With the Senate passage three weeks later, the bill made its way to Gov. Booth Gardner.[67]

On April 3, 1986, at the historic site of the Nippon Kan facility in Seattle, with the former clerks standing behind him and an exuberant audience of supporters in front, Gardner signed the bill into law. Punctuated by spontaneous cheers, speeches were made by Gary Locke, Art Wang, T. J. Vassar, and Sally Shimanaka Kazama. In the midst of the celebration, Mako Nakagawa hugged May Namba, who, after 41 years, had just been hired back to work for the Seattle School District.

7 / Determination

Be brief, concise and to the point. You may not always have all the time you want to explain all the ramifications of your issue to someone you want to influence. . . . So, develop and practice your brief (one to three minutes) version of a "sales talk" by including the "why, who, what, when, how" in the first few sentences. Identify yourself and your affiliation. Be respectful but not obsequious, determined but not adamant.
—"Techniques for Effective Advocacy: Lobbying Skills"[1]

Lobbying is difficult, pleading your case, holding your hat in your hand. I didn't enjoy it.
—Chuck Kato[2]

CONGRESSIONAL REDRESS BILLS

As the Washington Coalition on Redress worked to pass the state-level redress bills, U.S. Rep. Mike Lowry waited impatiently for the Commission on Wartime Relocation and Internment of Civilians to issue its recommendations so that he could resubmit his redress bill. "In fact," Cherry Kinoshita said, "we had to restrain him, telling him his bill would have a much better chance if it matched the commission's recommendations, so he reluctantly held off."

Once the commission had released its recommendations, WCR and Lowry burst into action. It was imperative to WCR that Lowry start the ball rolling immediately. National-level redress had stalled during the term of the commission, and with the extremely favorable commission recommendations now being released, there was no reason to delay. Chuck Kato thought it important that Lowry introduce his bill as soon as he could, while the CWRIC recommendations were still fresh in people's minds.

Only a week after the commission published its recommendations, on June 16, 1983, Lowry introduced H.R. 3387, the World War II Civil Liberties Violation Redress Act. Incorporating the findings of the commission, the language of Lowry's bill allocated $20,000 per "eligible individual," defined as

> any individual of Japanese or Alaskan Aleut ancestry who was enrolled on the records of the United States Government during the period beginning December 7, 1941, and ending on December 17, 1944, as being in a prohibited military zone, or confined, held in custody, or otherwise deprived of liberty or property[3]

as a result of Executive Order 9066 and Public Law 503, which made it illegal for citizens to disobey a military order in a military zone, and other governmental acts.

In addition, Lowry's bill stated that unclaimed redress payments would be used to fund "community services or assistance (including educational, health, housing, cultural, and similar services) in areas of the United States which are populated by eligible individuals or their descendants." Since payments would be made subject to congressional budget authorizations, the payments would be issued in order of the recipients' dates of birth, with the oldest persons receiving full payment first.

Twenty-four co-sponsors, including Rep. Norman Mineta (D-California), signed on to the bill, which was referred to the House Judiciary Committee's Subcommittee on Administrative Law and Governmental Relations. Sen. Alan Cranston (D-California) introduced a similar bill in the Senate.

As soon as Lowry introduced H.R. 3387, WCR began contacting members of the state's congressional delegation. Kinoshita had been appointed to the board of JACL's Legislative Education Committee (JACL / LEC, the organization's lobbying arm), and during the summer she made several phone calls to the office of Rep. Tom Foley of Spokane. In August, Foley became the first representative to agree to support Lowry's bill.[4]

Others simply ignored it or had decided to wait; many knew that another redress bill was in the works. Sponsored by House Majority Leader Jim Wright (D-Texas) and drafted by Mineta staff member Glen Roberts, the bill's purpose was also "to accept the findings and to implement the recommendations of the Commission on Wartime Relocation and Internment of Civilians." Wright's bill followed the recommendations of the CWRIC report more closely, asking that a fund of $1.5 billion be created, from which restitutions of $20,000 would be disbursed to each eligible Japanese American. In addition, a fund of $5 million would be created for Aleuts, from which a restitution of $5,000 would be paid to each eligible individual. Also included in the bill was a congressional apology, as recommended in the CWRIC report.

By late summer, when the introduction of the Wright / Mineta bill became a strong likelihood, Lowry called on his co-signers to transfer their support to it. When the bill was introduced in Congress, on October 6, 1983, as the Civil Liberties Act of 1983 (H.R. 4110), there were 73 sponsors, with Wright as the prime sponsor. Reps. Foley, Long, Lowry, Mineta, Matsui, and Rodino were the principal co-sponsors, and there were 66 additional co-sponsors, 44 of whom had signed on to Lowry's H.R. 3387. Wright's bill, H.R. 4110, was assigned to the House Judiciary Committee.[5]

In November, Sen. Spark Matsunaga of Hawaii introduced the Senate version, S. 2116, with 13 co-sponsors. The bill was assigned to the Senate Governmental Affairs Committee. By April 1984, both of Washington's senators, Dan Evans and Slade Gorton, had agreed to co-sponsor S. 2116. The congressmen presented a far more reluctant group. Rep. Rod Chandler supported the commission's suggestion that Congress apologize for the internment, but he had reservations about the $20,000 compensation. "While the value of such compensation as an act of recognition should not be underestimated," Chandler wrote to Ken Nakano in June, "Congress must consider the costs of any new program. The House Judiciary Committee plans to hold hearings on this issue in June. I am confident that appropriate legislation will be enacted, and as Congress considers this matter, I will keep your views in mind."[6] Rep. Al Swift, writing to Mayme (Semba) Nishimura, expressed similar sentiments:

> The aspect of the proposed redress that involves the payment of money troubles me a great deal. I have [struggled] and continue to struggle with the merits. I understand its symbolic importance to many who were interned. I am revolted by the racism that drips from some of the letters that I receive that oppose any redress at all. But, at least to date, I cannot persuade myself that this aspect of the redress is appropriate. It seems to me that it smacks of "buying our way out" of what must certainly be a matter of national conscience.[7]

Swift and Chandler were typical of U.S. representatives who were not yet willing to support redress, although not one of them defended the incarceration as a "military necessity," at least not openly.

By the end of the 98th Congress, there were 107 co-sponsors of H.R. 4110. The Judiciary Subcommittee on Administrative Law and Governmental Relations did hold hearings on the bill, but Rep. Sam Hall, committee chair, considered the bill a low priority, and it languished. Likewise, in the other house of Congress, Sen. Matsunaga's bill, S. 2116, received only one hearing— in Los Angeles, with the Governmental Affairs Subcommittee on Civil Service, Post Office and General Services—and died in committee (at the end of the 98th Congress, S. 2116 had 20 co-sponsors).

With the convening of the 99th Congress, the Civil Liberties Act, this time symbolically assigned the number 442, in honor of the well-decorated, mostly Nisei 442nd Regimental Combat Team, was reintroduced in the House on January 3, 1985, with 99 sponsors. Matsunaga's bill was reintroduced in the Senate on May 2, 1985, as S. 1053.[8]

At the end of the 98th Congress, Foley and Lowry had been the only Washington members of the House of Representatives who openly supported redress. But in the November 1984 elections, John Miller, a Republican radio news commentator, was elected. As a commentator, Miller had publicly supported local redress, and as a candidate he had supported national redress. Upon taking office, in 1985, he immediately signed on as a co-sponsor.[9]

Another early convert was Rep. Sid Morrison, a Republican representing Washington's 4th congressional district, a rural fruit-orchard region that also included the Hanford Nuclear Works project, an area known to be conservative. Karen Seriguchi, by then regional director of JACL's Pacific Northwest District, had written to Morrison and asked him to co-sponsor Lowry's H.R. 3387. Morrison's answer was noncommittal: "I feel it is necessary to take all factors into consideration before making a final decision on this issue, and I will not cosponsor Congressman Lowry's bill until I have had a chance to study the Commission's final document."[10]

However, in 1984, a Morrison constituent, Kara Kondo, coordinated an impressive lobbying effort of petitions and letters. She set up a spring 1985 meeting with Morrison for Kinoshita and Tim Otani, who had succeeded Seriguchi as JACL's Pacific Northwest District regional director. These efforts helped Morrison make his decision, in May 1985, to support redress. Kinoshita later wrote:

> As [Morrison] sat down to talk with us, he said in effect, let's see if you can convince me. We all gave the usual reasons for supporting redress—then I

happened to think of a professor who was doing a research project with Japanese Americans in Seattle who had had reservations about individual monetary redress at the outset, but by the conclusion of the study, which dealt with the mental health of hundreds of Nisei, she became convinced that individual monetary redress was appropriate and necessary for the healing process. I related this to the congressman and paused, thinking, Well, we gave it a try. Surprisingly, then, after some discussion he said, "I guess I'll be like your researcher. I can change my views and I agree to support your bill." I mentally danced a little jig.[11]

The fall of 1986 brought good news. In the November election, Brock Adams defeated the incumbent, Sen. Slade Gorton, and immediately signed on as a co-sponsor of Matsunaga's bill. Adams's support stemmed from his days as a student at Broadway High School, in Seattle, where Japanese American had made up two-thirds of the student body until the spring of 1942. Adams had also been a longtime friend and admirer of Rep. Patsy Mink, Sen. Daniel Inouye, and Matsunaga, three Nikkei members of Congress.[12]

In the House, Barney Frank of Massachusetts, an ardent supporter of redress who had studied the *Korematsu* case in law school,[13] assumed the chair of the Administrative Law and Governmental Relations Subcommittee of the House Judiciary Committee, replacing Rep. Dan Glickman of Kansas. With Frank as chair, redress activists knew the bill was more likely to move out of subcommittee and pass out of the full Judiciary Committee.

WCR continued, with unrelenting face-to-face meetings, to lobby for the support of other representatives as it became likely that there would be a vote on H.R. 442 in 1987. Some community activists, such as Chizu Omori, Hiro Nishimura, and Miyo Kaneta, took the initiative and wrote letters to nearly all the members of the state's congressional delegation, urging support. Still others spent countless hours on indirect lobbying, meeting with groups and legislators' constituents and appearing before press and media. Chuck Kato, Cherry Kinoshita, Wayne Kimura, Ken Nakano, Hiro Nishimura, Peter Okada, Chizu Omori, Bob Sato, Sam Shoji, Theresa Takayoshi, and Massie Tomita led the public education efforts, keeping the redress movement in the public eye. Their efforts also helped raise funds to carry on the lobbying.

During the same period, between 1983 and 1986, Seattle activists also were working on the *coram nobis* case of Gordon Hirabayashi and on the suit that had been brought by the National Council for Japanese American Redress.[14] Washingtonians were bombarded with the stories of Japanese Americans, their eviction from the West Coast (especially from the Puget Sound area), and their incarceration.

At this time WCR, the Seattle Chapter JACL, and JACL's Pacific Northwest District worked more in sync with the national JACL, which supported a nationwide coordinated effort, and its Legislative Education Committee; the JACL/LEC raised over a million dollars to support the national lobbying.

Also working together in this coordinated effort were the Nisei veterans groups. The Nisei Veterans Committee (NVC), which earlier had given SERC such a hard time, officially supported redress in 1981, but its attitudes had already changed by the 1978 Day of Remembrance; the group had been instrumental in getting National Guard support for the motorcade and trucks.[15] As part of the WCR, the NVC offered the use of its building for numerous redress events, including the mock commission hearings and a showing of the videotaped hearings.[16] Art Susumi of the American Legion Cathay Post #186 worked with the Cathay Post's delegates to the state convention, Jackson Pang and Calvin Fung, to halt a resolution against redress proposed by Vernon Hill of the Puyallup Post, who was urging the American Legion to oppose the $20,000 redress compensation and apology to Japanese Americans. Hill's effort died in the American Legion's resolutions committee when the chair decided not to permit it a full-membership vote.

The effects of lobbying, both direct and indirect, could be seen in the cases of Reps. Don Bonker, Al Swift, and Rod Chandler. The conversion of Bonker, from southwest Washington, could be traced from his replies to requests and meetings, which slowly changed as he was "educated" by WCR and constituents. The letters from 1985 to 1986 show that the representative started out noncommittal:

> While I understand that this is the intent of part of this legislation, I do, however, have some concerns about the impact of the $1.5 billion dollar trust fund that would be set up under H.R. 442 in order to provide those affected with limited compensation. It is for this reason that I have withheld my cosponsorship so far.[17]

> [M]y problem with this legislation has always been a concern about the budget implications of the provisions for financial restitution to surviving internees. It has been for this reason that I have not joined as a cosponsor.

As for your question regarding my support for the bill should it come to the floor of the House, I am reluctant to commit myself on a measure such as this which could well be amended before it even comes for a vote.[18]

After several failed attempts to get Bonker's support, a chance meeting at a Lowry fundraiser provided WCR with an opening. As Kinoshita reported,

One had to keep alert for opportunities, with attendance at political gatherings a must since they provided a potential source for meeting specific congressmen. At a fund-raising shrimp feed for Mike Lowry, we spotted Rep. Don Bonker, who had resisted any commitment even after two visits with him, so we decided to corner him and try again. This time, as usual, he gave his "budget deficit" excuses. Then when we told him that since the bill was ready for the Rules Committee, that was why it was important to line up the votes, he said, "You don't have to worry about that."

With that small glimmer of hope, I persisted with his district office manager until an arrangement was made for the congressman to meet with us at the Elliott Bay Bookstore, one of his campaign stops [in Seattle]. While Chuck Kato, Tim Gojio, and I waited at a small table, Rep. Bonker walked in, asked a few questions about where the money was to come from, and then spoke in somewhat ambiguous terms. We looked at each other as we realized that he was agreeing to support the bill.

Still a little dubious, I asked for a confirming letter. He said, "Here, I'll write it on this card," and he then proceeded to handwrite, "This is to inform you that I intend to vote in favor of H.R. 442 when it reaches the House floor later this year," and dated it, "Aug. 12, 1987."[19]

Bonker would go on to clarify his position on the redress bill the following month, saying that although his intention was not to co-sponsor the bill because of its "budget implications," he did intend to support it "should it come before the full House for consideration."[20]

From early on, the argument of Al Swift, the representative from Washington's second district, had been a little puzzling to WCR. As Kinoshita wrote,

Although Rep. Swift was truly sincere, he had trouble articulating his almost passionate objections to the individual monetary compensation. In a letter which I had asked him to write outlining his objections, he referred to "trivializing" the enormity of the event by "conscience money." That initiated from several of us deeply introspective responses to his rationale.[21]

However, on July 2, 1987, a year later, when WCR met with Swift for the fourth time, he finally agreed to support the monetary compensation, apologizing for his "glacial" progress. In a follow-up letter of July 16 to Kinoshita, he confirmed: "I can now tell you that I have resolved the concerns on which we've had many conversations. . . . Combined with the long communication with you, your group and me, they have persuaded me the balance on this issue favors the legislation as reported from the Committee."

While Swift credited Rep. Doris Matsui and the WCR with persuading him, he also wrote, in later correspondence,

> I was sitting next to Doris at one of the tables. While the others chatted, I said, "Doris, I need some help," and I explained my reservations. She explained, again, the view of Japanese Americans. I reiterated my reluctance to "buy out" the guilt for the actions of our government. Finally, at the same old impasse, I said something about just not being able to find a good reason to support the payment portion of the bill. And then Doris said, very quietly, referring to so many of the victims, that, "Maybe the best reason to support it is just that then, it will be finally over."
>
> In my memory, her statement changed my mind in that instant.
>
> Doris' statement changed my focus from what I wanted uninvolved Americans to feel about the facts perpetrated in their name, to focus on the victims of those actions. With that new focus, I began to rethink the issue and, finally, I was able to vote for the bill. In fact, I came to support it with conviction—because it could bring closure to those who had been hurt. Further, I suppose my view that there needed to be a profound recognition by Americans of how truly un-American those historic actions were, was naive.[22]

Of all the Washington delegation, Rep. Chandler was the most difficult to convince, deciding to vote for H.R. 442 the day before the final House vote. Kinoshita, Tomio Moriguchi, and Tom Gojio met with Chandler in late summer. Chandler was still reluctant. Kinoshita asked if his position could be characterized as "qualified support." Chandler answered, "Before you quote me and give the wrong impression, just say to your group that you went away disappointed."[23] As the three lobbyists got up to leave, Kinoshita, "in last-minute desperation," turned to Chandler and said, "When it comes time to vote, please remember that if for no other reason, you should vote for the redress bill because it's the right thing to do."

Unsure whether the congressman would heed her words, Kinoshita later watched the congressional debate on television:

> On C-SPAN, as the House debate progressed, there was Rep. Chandler at the podium saying, "I have thought about this with my mind for a long time, and until this week I was undecided, but when I turned to my heart I realized this is what has got to be done. . . . Let us do it because it is ultimately the right thing to do."[24]

On September 17, 1987, the 200th anniversary of the signing of the U.S. Constitution, the House of Representatives debated and passed H.R. 442, with 243 members voting for redress and 141 against. A few months later, in April 1988, the U.S. Senate passed the redress bill by a 69–27 vote. It would be August before a joint House / Senate committee would agree to a final version of the bill. But the hard work and dedication of the Washington Coalition on Redress could be seen in the impressive final tally on the Civil Liberties Act among members of the Washington State congressional delegation: 10 yes, 0 no.[25]

President Ronald Reagan signed the Civil Liberties Act on August 10, 1988, but the elation was short-lived. By statute, payments would be based on annual congressional appropriations. Ronald Reagan, in his final budget proposal before leaving office, earmarked $20 million for redress, enough to compensate only 1,000 out of an estimated 80,000 persons eligible for redress. As the budget proposal worked its way through various committees in Congress, the figure vacillated wildly: $250 million in April 1989, $150 million in May (Senate and House), $50 million in September (House).

On September 29, Sen. Inouye, although initially a lukewarm supporter of redress, proposed to the Senate that, in return for a one-year delay in the initiation of payments, redress under the Civil Liberties Act become an entitlement program (with guaranteed funding) rather than an appropriation (with annual budgetary approval). Thanks to Inouye's political muscle, acquired over his 27 years in the Senate, the 1990 appropriations bill, which included Inouye's provision, sailed through Congress in October and was signed by President George Bush on November 21. Thus, although no redress payments would be made in fiscal year 1990, payments were guaranteed to begin in fiscal year 1991.

REDRESS SUPERSTARS

As the Civil Liberties Act required, the oldest eligible individuals were paid first. The payments to Seattle centenarians occurred on October 14, 1990. At the Nisei Veterans Hall, with standing room only, Harry Nakagawa (100 years old), Kichisaburo Ishimitsu (103), Uta Wakamatsu (102), Shoichiro Katsuno (105), and Frank Yatsu (107) received their $20,000 checks and presidential apologies. The Office of Redress Administration,[26] recognizing volunteers who had been especially helpful in sponsoring redress workshops and educating the public about the redress program, presented awards to the WCR / Seattle Chapter JACL core group of redress activists: Chuck Kato, Cherry Kinoshita, Wayne Kimura, Ken Nakano, Chizu Omori, Bob Sato, Sam Shoji, and Massie Tomita. Henry Miyatake, Shosuke Sasaki, and Mike Nakata also attended and were introduced to the gathering as the pioneers of the redress bill. Chuck Kato, asked by a community reporter about redress passage, said simply that redress had been "a long time coming."[27]

8 / Arrival

If you had to say what's the one reason of the redress legislation passing,
it was because of the Seattle Chapter JACL. There are many other people,
but they are the driving force that made it happen.

—Mike Lowry[1]

A large, framed American flag dominates the back wall of the front room of
the Seattle Chapter JACL office. Attached to the flag in the frame is a photograph of President Reagan signing the Civil Liberties Act of 1988. To the group
of legislators assembled with the president, this was a joyous occasion, the
successful conclusion of a campaign that few had believed possible 20 or even
10 years earlier.

But one face is noticeably missing from that photograph: the face of
Mike Lowry. Although Lowry carried the Seattle plan to Congress and was
instrumental in the most noted characteristic of the Civil Liberties Act—
monetary payments to individuals forcibly evicted or incarcerated during
World War II—he was not present at the signing.[2]

The individual redress payments were the symbol of the government's
apology. While much of the Seattle Evacuation Redress Committee's original plan did not survive legal scrutiny and political expediency, its core—
individual payments—remained intact. The fund for educational purposes,
the provision that payments to eligible recipients start with the eldest first,
and the stipulation that the U.S. attorney general be responsible for identi-
fying and locating each eligible individual (without requiring any application for payment from eligible recipients, and using records already in the
possession of the United States government) also withstood modifications
to the bill.

Other, earlier redress plans had focused on block grants or trust funds to be used to educate the public about the incarceration, rebuild the Japanese American community, or improve U.S.–Japan relations. Therefore, Seattle's redress activists are convinced that without "Henry's plan" (the plan developed by Henry Miyatake), there would be no redress, at least in the form of direct monetary compensation to individuals.

Clifford Uyeda and Peggy Nagae, members of JACL's National Reparations Committee in 1977–78, echoed this sentiment. In response to questions about SERC, Uyeda, originally from Tacoma, wrote, "I was proud of the independent thinking of the Pacific Northwest; they were the original thinkers on many issues affecting Japanese Americans. The concept of redress was only talked about elsewhere; people in Seattle acted on the concept with specific ideas. I liked their spirit."[3]

Nagae, at a recent redress conference, was a little more blunt: "Henry, Chuck [Kato], Shosuke [Sasaki], the Seattle folks—they were the ones who really got it started. They kicked us in the butt until we did something."

The Seattle Evacuation Redress Committee was the first group to offer a concrete redress proposal for the Nikkei community and its supporters. SERC conducted one of the earliest polls about redress, to find out what Japanese Americans felt about the forced evacuation, the incarceration, and redress. SERC also produced the "Appeal for Action" (see Appendix 1), an effective effort to educate the Nikkei community about basic constitutional rights. This effort, according to Seattleites, brought pressure on the national JACL to act on mandates from the governing body, and it forced action by the reluctant Nikkei members of Congress, who proposed, instead of redress, the Commission on Wartime Relocation and Internment of Civilians.

Seattle redress activists organized and produced media events and newsworthy texts of interest to local and national media. The Seattle Chapter JACL Cultural Committee's mounting of the *Pride and Shame* exhibit in 1971, the "Appeal for Action," the 1978 Day of Remembrance, the Community Committee on Redress / Reparation's 1981 mock hearing and the subsequent CWRIC hearings, the Seattle / Puyallup JACL chapters' 1983 erection of the Puyallup monument, the Washington Coalition on Redress's campaigns for redress at the city, state, and national levels—all of these helped to educate the public about the World War II expulsion and imprisonment and maximized media coverage.

Perhaps understandably, Seattle activists are certain that, at the very least, the Civil Liberties Act of 1988 had its roots in Seattle. At the October 1988 victory celebration at the Nisei Veterans Hall, Mike Lowry presented to the

Seattle Chapter JACL the flag that had flown over Congress the day the Civil Liberties Act was signed. More than 300 people attended the celebration, titled to leave no doubt about how its organizers felt: "Celebrate for Redress: Born in Seattle":

> In the latter stages, the old nuts-and-bolts, grind-it-out lobbying, vote getting, that's not too creative. The uniqueness of [Seattle's approach] lies in how grassroots people learned about how the American government really works. It doesn't work like a people's government. A lot is boring, not glamorous. Unheroic. The group in Washington took on redress and went from beginning to end. It was largely successful because someone had a plan. You need a plan. The Seattle people had one.[4]

SEATTLE: READY FOR REDRESS

> What struck me most about Seattle was how militant the Nisei are
> (a desirable trait in my eyes), how active they are politically, and how
> closely they work with Native Americans, Hispanics, Jews, Blacks, and
> other community groups.
>
> —Karen Seriguchi[5]

The redress story is a combination fairy tale, morality play, and underdog-pulling-off-a-monumental-upset story. In these stories, the protagonist endures extreme suffering, works hard, overcomes all obstacles, and reaches a goal. To explain what happens is to explain the inexplicable. It just happens. And it does because all the elements are in place.

This is not to say that the redress movement would have never begun elsewhere, that such a movement won't happen again, or that there is a formula by which we can make it happen all the time.

Redress began in Seattle. There was a man with a plan and a group that liked, understood, and developed his plan. That talented group expanded its membership. Its plan, conceived and nurtured in the right circumstances, soared and flew away to be claimed by all:

> Henry Miyatake made a Cleveland kit glider when he was a boy in camp. "I spent a lot of time on it," he said. . . . "I worked very diligently on it, and painted it. And I guess, I made it too good. I flew it, and it just kept going. The last I saw of it, it was heading toward Hazelton, Idaho."[6]

Miyatake began his quest during a period in which an awakening of ethnic pride among minorities had forced the issue of race relations to the forefront of the nation's consciousness. In the Seattle area, this growing awareness did not escape the Asian American community.[7]

Because of Seattle's early restrictive housing laws, many of the area's Asian and African Americans had grown up together, forming friendships and political alliances. Cross-racial, cross-ethnic ties were created early. The support group for minority state workers that included Ruth Woo, Ron Sims, Tim Gojio, Frankie Irigon, Naomi Iwata-Sanchez, and others was not unique; it was repeated in other areas of employment (for example, in the Asian Coalition for Equality, the Minority Executive Directors Coalition, the Asian Pacific Directors Coalition, the Northwest Labor and Employment Law Office, and the Cannery Workers Union). This cohesiveness, especially on issues of concern to minorities, translated into effective grassroots lobbying. Sen. George Fleming, the only nonwhite male in the state Senate, felt an expanded sense of constituency encompassing not only those in his district but also women and other minorities.[8] T. J. Vassar was interested in the case of the school clerks not only because he believed that compensating them was the right thing to do but also because of his own personal experiences: he knew Mako Nakagawa personally, and he lived in the same neighborhood as Nakagawa and a few of the former clerks; seeing them in the neighborhood grocery store or on neighborhood walks personalized their stories for him.[9]

The effective organizing of the Asian American community around political issues in the 1970s (notably, the building of the Kingdome and Interstate 5, which physically split the International District) awakened city, county, and state politicians to the emerging clout of the Asian Americans, the largest minority group in King County. It also groomed future Asian American leaders for the political arena. But circumstances such as these do not guarantee success in passing a bill. To judge by the comments of those who supported the Japanese American community, the forces driving the redress campaign were the community itself and the rightness of the cause.

No one was better qualified to speak for the rightness of redress than those who had experienced the expulsion and incarceration. The same media events that informed the general American populace also developed and enlarged the pool of speakers willing to talk about their wartime experiences. Each event, large or small, contributed to the awakening of a community that, until then, had focused on rebuilding individual lives. Soon the Japanese American community in Seattle had a well-informed body that could lobby effectively on local fronts. Lobbying skills learned during the city and state redress efforts, whether in grassroots lobbying (educating the electorate) or face-to-face lobbying (holding direct meetings with legislators), were refined and used at the national level.

Mike Lowry, asked about the possibility of CWRIC's returning a report unfavorable to redress, had said, "I don't see how it's possible that reasonable men could look at the facts and not come to the conclusion that a great injustice was done and that some meaningful legislation is necessary to correct that act."[10] For most activists, this was a given. They were kept going by the belief that the American public, given the truth about the expulsion and incarceration, would support their campaign, and in the end the rightness of redress was a major reason for the support of public officials, not only Rep. Rod Chandler but others as well, from Charles Z. Smith, Dan Evans, and Jim Dolliver to George Fleming, Gary Locke, Art Wang, and the state's entire congressional delegation.

What about redress? Did it bring the respect that Henry Miyatake so fervently wanted for the Nikkei community?

> Seventeen years passed from the time Miyatake brought his plan to the local chapter of the JACL to the distribution of an apology letter and monetary redress to surviving victims. Through these years, the opinions of most Japanese Americans were almost completely reversed. In the early 1970s, redress and even camp experiences were taboo subjects. Today, to say "Let's just forget about camp" has become unacceptable. Now one Sansei leader describes it as almost "fashionable" to talk about camp and redress.[11]

There is general agreement that the campaign itself brought about respect for Japanese Americans. The mostly favorable media coverage reflected and encouraged the general populace's acknowledgment of the internment. As a result, the expulsion and incarceration are part of American history. To Cherry Kinoshita, this is the most important thing the campaign accomplished:

> It no longer surprises me when in the course of discussion with non-Japanese doctors, attorneys, accountants, etc., they nod knowingly when I speak of the 3–4 years [I spent] away from Seattle "courtesy of the government." As long as schools ask for speakers to tell about camp and the internment, we can feel that the education efforts are lasting.[12]

The campaign for redress also played an important role in unifying a community whose generations had been torn apart by World War II. It enabled Nikkei to talk not only to legislative bodies, the media, and the greater American community but, just as important, to other Nikkei generations as well. Commented Miyatake,

> I dare say that Nihonjin [people of Japanese ancestry] came out of the closet. That's the result of redress, the Day of Remembrance, and all those events. I think these guys were able to come out of the closet and tell the stories to their kids, their grandchildren. The commission, [despite the fact] that I had opposed it, was a lot of good, because of the exposure of information that created a wealth of ideas that were generated by these people. [They were able to say] "Okay, I'm willing to speak about it," but up until then, they were reticent.[13]

And what about the $20,000 payments, the most tangible aspect of redress? Was the amount significant enough? For those who argue the benefits of redress, it was; others have reservations.

Rep. Al Swift voted for the Civil Liberties Act because, he hoped, it would bring closure to the Japanese Americans who were incarcerated. He felt and still feels that no sum was large enough to really compensate for the incarceration; the $20,000 he voted for represented closure, not compensation, and, a decade after redress had passed, he asked if Japanese Americans now felt a sense of closure.[14]

Many of those who argue the benefits of redress report that they do now feel a sense of closure, at least with the United States government, but others remain unsatisfied. A Seattle Nisei who wished to remain anonymous was emphatic in answering Swift's question: "I was against redress then, and I'm against redress now. There's no sum high enough that could compensate. And I don't want closure. I want people to remember the horror of what was done, every minute of every day. There should never be closure."

In the Nisei Wartime Internment Research Project, a study of Nisei attitudes, research psychologist Donna Nagata reported that 30 percent of her sample felt redress did result in a sense of closure over the evacuation-and-internment segment of their lives, 30 percent did not, and 40 percent felt varying degrees of closure. Some felt, like the Seattle Nisei, that no sum would have been high enough, but what bothered many was that redress had come too late for most of the Issei, and so there could never be any closure.[15]

Henry Miyatake remains uneasy about another aspect—the Supreme Court rulings on the curfew, expulsion, and incarceration still stand:

> I wanted to change the Supreme Court decision. That was one of the fundamental things I wanted to do, and we still have not done that. The District Court of Appeals has taken it on as a final decision point [and] the Supreme Court refused to acknowledge the hearing on the total issue, so the law still stands as a part of American history and judicial process. And the Congress itself, even though they made some apology in the bill that they passed and Reagan signed, did not entirely revoke Public Law 503 that they passed in March 1942. They did not do that.[16]

In a sense, this story has returned to its beginning. Miyatake still feels there is unfinished business. After all, it was not just respect he was working for; it was justice for all Americans, current and future. The plan fell a little short of his hopes, although it succeeded well beyond his expectations.

APPENDIX 1

An Appeal for Action to Obtain Redress for the World War II

Evacuation and Imprisonment of Japanese Americans

Among the documents which form the philosophical and legal foundations of our nation, such as The Declaration of Independence and The Constitution of the United States of America, no idea is more basic in the origin and development of American history, traditions and statutes than the principle of equality of all persons before the law. Even the most cursory study of our nation's history leads to the inescapable conclusion that in the opinion of the Founding Fathers, such as Franklin, Adams and Jefferson, true Americanism meant an unbending insistence by each individual that any government accord him equality of treatment before its laws and refrain from unjustly violating certain "unalienable rights" such as "life, liberty and the pursuit of happiness."

Over thirty years ago, a few months after the entry of the United States into World War II, the Government of the United States without a shred of evidence of misconduct or disloyalty and without even a pretense of a trial, perpetrated the wholesale uprooting and imprisonment of practically all Pacific Coast residents of Japanese ancestry. True, the Government did not engage in systematic murder of Japanese Americans, but it did callously dispossess us of practically all the rest of our rights such as the right to a fair trial, liberty, our jobs, our businesses, and our homes. This monstrous violation of the most basic of American traditions and laws relating to human freedom was the culmination of four decades of anti-Japanese propaganda of the most vile, outrageous and pervasive sort, particularly in the newspapers printed in the Pacific Coast states.

This propaganda brain-washed the mass of white Americans into feeling that the Japanese were subhuman creatures deserving of no rights whatever and brainwashed the Japanese Americans into thinking that they had been born of an unworthy race and that they had to submit meekly to practically any governmental trampling of their human rights in order to "prove" to others that the Nisei were "loyal Americans." The fact that even after a lapse of thirty years no real attempt has been made by Japanese Americans to obtain redress for the wrongs, humiliations and loss of income suffered by them during their totally unwarranted imprisonment indicates that the older Nisei at least, have been so psychologically crippled by their pre-war and wartime experience that they have been unable to act as Americans should.

Passive submission or self-abasement when confronted by government tyranny or injustice was alien to the beliefs held by the founders of this nation. If, in the face of British government tyranny, they had acted like the Nisei have in the face of American government tyranny, there would be no 200th Anniversary of the founding of our country to celebrate. In commemorating the birth of our nation, therefore, it is time that Americans of Japanese ancestry repudiate the pseudo-American doctrine, promoted by white racists and apparently believed in by some former Nisei leaders, that there is one kind of Americanism for whites and another kind for non-whites. If Japanese Americans are as American as the J.A.C.L. has often claimed, then they should act like Americans and make every effort to seek redress through legislation and the courts for the rape of almost all their "unalienable rights" by the United States Government over thirty years ago.

Judging from the polls taken on the attitudes of the people living in the Pacific Northwest areas and the quantity of anti-Japanese hate mail and phone calls to local television stations immediately following programs dealing honestly with the evacuation and incarceration of Japanese Americans, over half of the white population of those areas believe to this day that the World War II treatment of the Japanese Americans was justified and that there was truth in the charges against us of espionage and sabotage.

By custom and tradition, any American who has been injured as a result of false accusations is expected to bring those responsible into court and obtain a judgment clearing his name and awarding him monetary damages from the offending parties. Failure by the slandered or libeled person to take legal action against his accusers is often regarded by the public as an indication that the charges are true.

When Japanese Americans obviously have done nothing against those who systematically vilified and libeled them during the first half of this century;

have meekly submitted to mass imprisonment by the Government without receiving a formal statement of charges or a trial; and, thereafter have failed thus far even to ask for redress from the Government for that unjustified imprisonment, the white majority living on the Pacific Coast can hardly be blamed for looking upon the Japanese Americans as actually having been espionage agents and saboteurs at the start of World War II.

No amount of docile submission to white officials or "demonstrations of loyalty" to the United States by the Nisei can ever "disprove" the false accusations in the minds of most white Americans. That can only be done when the Government of the United States either through Congress or through its courts publicly declares that the wartime uprooting and imprisonment of Japanese Americans was totally without justification and awards the victims of its wartime outrage proper and reasonable redress.

Government recognition of and payment for wrongs done to their ancestors several generations ago have been secured by a number of Native American Indian tribes and Alaskan Natives in recent years. There can be little doubt that someday Americans of Japanese descent will press for and obtain reparations for the World War II uprooting and imprisonment of the Issei and Nisei. And while it is better to obtain redress of wrongs even generations late than not at all, for most Issei, justice delayed would in effect mean justice denied. In fact, many of the Issei who were most seriously hurt by the evacuation and imprisonment are already dead and gone and within five or ten years most of the remaining Issei will have passed away. Even some of the older Nisei are starting to die in slowly increasing numbers.

Except for approximately 10% of the Nisei who are convinced that they "have it made" or have been "accepted by the whites" and are opposed to any action which would "rock the boat," there is general agreement among Japanese Americans that action to obtain redress for the evacuation and related injustices is needed. Recent surveys show that a heavy majority want any payments made directly to each individual claimant. The surveys also reveal almost total agreement that the Issei should be given first priority in receiving such payments.

If redress and justice are to be gotten for the Issei and Nisei, strong and determined efforts must immediately be initiated and pushed to a successful conclusion. Most Americans believe in justice and it is unlikely that their elected officials in the United States Government would now deny a just settlement if the true facts of our unjustified maltreatment at the hands of the Government during World War II were properly presented.

In seeking redress, the nature of injuries and losses for which we hope to obtain monetary compensation must first be understood. Through the provisions of the Evacuation Claims Bill which was signed into law in 1948, former evacuees received (after legal and processing fees) a total net payment of $34,200,000 as "compensation" for their property losses which were estimated by the Federal Reserve Bank of San Francisco at $400,000,000 in 1942. Under the terms of those payments, we now are precluded from asking for a more just settlement for losses of property. Our present efforts, therefore, are directed toward obtaining redress for other injuries and losses.

For the mental and emotional suffering at the time of the evacuation and the psychological injuries sustained from the exile from their homes no fair compensation in dollars can be computed. Almost equally impossible would be any attempt to place a dollar value on the educational losses inflicted on the Japanese Americans of school age by the sudden termination of their normal schooling and by the Government's suppression of the teaching of the Japanese language and certain branches of Japanese culture. On the basis of recent court awards to persons subjected to unjustified imprisonment of even a few days, a payment of at least $5,000 to each person forced to leave his domicile as a result of the Evacuation Order in 1942 would appear to be appropriate. When the difficulties and costs to the evacuees in later settling in other areas of the country or in returning to their home areas on the Pacific Coast are also considered, the sum we suggest is far from excessive.

Furthermore, we believe that we are entitled to seek compensation from the Government for first, the prolonged loss of our personal liberty, second, for the loss of normal wage and salary incomes, and third, for the loss of business income for those who owned their businesses and farms. According to our estimates, based on 1942 dollars, the total wages and salaries lost by the Japanese Americans during their imprisonment was in excess of $400,000,000. No amounts for the value of lost pension rights, job seniority, lost opportunities for promotion, etc. are included in that figure. The total loss to Japanese Americans of the net incomes of businesses and farms which they were forced to leave behind as a result of their imprisonment is estimated by us to have amounted to over $200,000,000 in 1942 dollars. To cover these three classes of losses, we are suggesting a payment to each former inmate of those prison camps of $10 a day for each day of confinement, in addition to the flat payment of $5,000 already mentioned.

Two different methods for obtaining the money to pay these sums have been suggested. The first is the direct Congressional appropriations procedure with annual incremental appropriations over a period of years. An example of this method was the Evacuation Claims Bill. That Bill proved to be disappointing to Japanese Americans because of the inadequate provisions in the Bill, niggardly handling of the claims, and insufficient funds appropriated by Congress.

The other suggested method is the Bootstrap Concept (sometimes referred to as the Seattle Plan). This plan would require Congressional approval to set up an Internal Revenue Service Trust Fund which would receive Federal Income Taxes paid by persons of Japanese descent for a period of up to ten years or until all claims are satisfied. Almost simultaneously with the receipt of such taxes by the Fund, claims would be paid starting with the oldest Issei. The amount of money available each year would reflect the income taxes allocated voluntarily by those of Japanese descent. According to our estimates, over $200,000,000 would be available for claims disbursements each year. This method of funding would have the very important advantage of not being subject to the annual uncertainties of Congressional appropriations. It would also spare us from appearing to be pleading for Congressional handouts. The plan would include a basic stipulation which would prohibit those not allocating their taxes to the Fund from making any claims against the Fund.

Despite resolutions repeatedly passed at successive national J.A.C.L. conventions in favor of seeking reparations, a surprising succession of national officers and staff members have displayed a glacial reluctance to start any kind of effective moves toward such a goal. About their only contributions to discussions of the subject have been to emphasize the difficulties which would attend any such efforts.

In order to start a successful drive to get reparations, it is first of all necessary for the various J.A.C.L. chapter members to make it clearly known to the national J.A.C.L. officers and staff that action to seek redress must now be given top priority among the league's activities. Second, Japanese Americans must strive for and obtain public declarations of support for our goals from the greatest possible number of other organizations to which they belong such as churches, fraternal organizations, labor unions, civil rights groups, and political parties. And third, our position and the statements of those who support our efforts should unmistakably and repeatedly be brought to the attention of our Congressmen, Senators, and Officials of the Executive Branch of the Government.

The members of the Seattle Chapter of the J.A.C.L. earnestly ask for the help and cooperation of your organization in these efforts, not only to obtain justice in the form of reparation payments to the innocent victims of the World War II evacuation and imprisonment, but also to have the Government of the United States thereby demonstrate to the whole world that it still has the greatness of spirit to acknowledge and provide redress for its past miscarriages of justice. Such Government action would prove conclusively that the concept of the equality of all persons before the law, as conceived by the Founding Fathers, continues to remain a fundamental principle of our nation. And, that The Constitution of the United States of America even 200 years after its birth cannot be permanently set aside and ignored by government officials no matter what rank or post they may occupy.

Prepared by the editorial group
SHOSUKE SASAKI, Editor
MIKE NAKATA
HENRY J. MIYATAKE
Evacuation Redress Committee, Seattle J.A.C.L. Chapter
Approved for distribution by the Seattle J.A.C.L. Officers
and the Board of Directors
November 19, 1975

APPENDIX 2

An Open Letter to the Honorable S. I. Hayakawa

from Japanese America

Thirty-seven years ago, on February 19, 1942, forty years of race hatred exploded against "all persons of Japanese ancestry" in the form of a Presidential Executive Order. Franklin D. Roosevelt's Executive Order 9066 forced three generations of Nikkei out of our homes, birthplaces, businesses; made us give up, curtail, or abandon our property and education; deprived us of all civil rights; stigmatized us as "enemy aliens," legitimized the race hatred against us; and forced us into concentration camps, where most of us lived regimented lives behind barbed wire, under guard, for an average term of three years.

You, Senator Hayakawa, were not there with us on the West Coast, where the Issei, the first generation to arrive in America, established themselves as working, productive members of this country. You were not with us in the camps.

You have repeatedly, in the press, on radio and television, called the move for redressing the wrongs done to us and American justice "ridiculous and absurd." You have said we "weren't in prison camps," that they were "relocation centers." You credit the mass removal of Japanese Americans for breaking up our "ghettos" and for our higher education in "Antioch, Oberlin, the University of Chicago, Temple University, Mount Holyoke, and so on," and further credit the camps for giving us the opportunities that led to our enjoying the highest per capita income of any group in the nation.

They were concentration camps. Barbed wire, electrified fences, dogs, armed soldiers, machine gun towers made them concentration camps.

The colleges and universities you name are fine schools. We had been attending those schools years before WW II, and did not need the concentration camps to spark our academic achievement.

It was not our removal to camp that opened up the ghettos, but the repeal of anti-Oriental laws that barred the Issei from U.S. citizenship, owning property, and certain jobs. *After camp we had nothing.* That nothing is what camp gave us, not opportunity. It was hard work, combined with the help of a few good friends, that brought us our present success. That success does not make the concentration camps of yesterday any less heinous a violation of American justice. Our success does not excuse the camps from American history.

What you call the white hysteria of the time does not excuse or lessen the damage done to Japanese America or American justice. The Federal Reserve Bank assessed the value of our property lost in 1942 at $400 million. The Evacuation Claims Act of 1948 paid out a total of $38 million—9%. The redress we seek is not for property losses, but for the violation of civil rights, wrongful imprisonment, loss of income, and psychological, social, and cultural damages.

Japanese Americans were as outraged and shocked by the Japanese attack on Pearl Harbor as any other Americans, and as anxious to defend America. The need for revenge against the Japanese enemy in no way justified the willful mistaking of three generations of Japanese Americans for the foreign Japanese enemy.

In camp we maintained our faith in the justice of a nation that had broken faith with us. Our all-Nisei 442nd Regimental Combat Team fought in WW II with a distinction that made them the most decorated of any unit who fought in that awful war. With that same faith in American justice, we seek redress. What you have said about white backlash and forgetting the hardships we endured convinces us that—unless the concentration camps become a recognized and essential part of American history—our ideals and system are vulnerable to the very tyranny Americans loathe. The concentration camps can happen again.

From an obscure Canadian immigrant to a noted scholar, educator, and U.S. senator, you have become a prominent Japanese American. We regret that you choose now to make your reputation characterizing yourself as our "public enemy no. 1." You call yourself that as if the title brings you glory. In our eyes it does not. And on the concentration camps and our concern for redress, you do not speak for Japanese America.

The whites of today are different people. Today the mayors of cities that once called for our elimination are welcoming us home. In Seattle, Portland, San Francisco, and Los Angeles, the white establishment are joining four generations of Nikkei—Issei, Nisei, Sansei, and Yonsei—to remember, to heal, and to encourage the triumph of law. We firmly believe American law can heal itself. We look to you as one of the physicians and are saddened by your mouthing of the clichés of an ancient mob.

APPENDIX 3

An American Promise by the President

of the United States of America: A Proclamation

In this Bicentennial Year, we are commemorating the anniversary dates of many of the great events in American history. An honest reckoning, however, must include a recognition of our national mistakes as well as our national achievements. Learning from our mistakes is not pleasant, but as a great philosopher once admonished, we must do so if we want to avoid repeating them.

February 19th is the anniversary of a sad day in American history. It was on that date in 1942, in the midst of the response to the hostilities that began on December 7, 1941, that Executive Order No. 9066 was issued, subsequently enforced by the criminal penalties of a statute enacted March 21, 1942, resulting in the uprooting of loyal Americans. Over one hundred thousand persons of Japanese ancestry were removed from their homes, detained in special camps, and eventually relocated.

We now know what we should have known then—not only was that evacuation wrong, but Japanese-Americans were and are loyal Americans. On the battlefield and at home, Japanese-Americans—names like Hamada, Mitsumori, Marimoto, Noguchi, Yamasaki, Kido, Munemori and Miyamura—have been and continue to be written in our history for the sacrifices and the contributions they have made to the well-being and security of this, our common Nation.

The Executive order that was issued on February 19, 1942, was for the sole purpose of prosecuting the war with the Axis Powers, and ceased to be effective with the end of those hostilities. Because there was no formal statement of its termination, however, there is concern among many Japanese-Americans that there may yet be some life in that obsolete document. I think it appropriate, in this our Bicentennial Year, to remove all doubt on that matter, and to make clear our commitment in the future.

NOW, THEREFORE, I, GERALD FORD, President of the United States of America, do hereby proclaim that all the authority conferred by Executive Order No. 9066 terminated upon the issuance of Proclamation No. 2714, which formally proclaimed the cessation of the hostilities of World War II on December 31, 1946.

I call upon the American people to affirm with me this American Promise— that we have learned from the tragedy of that long-ago experience forever to treasure liberty and justice for each individual American, and resolve that this kind of action shall never again be repeated.

IN WITNESS WHEREOF, I have hereunto set my hand this nineteenth day of February in the year of our Lord nineteen hundred seventy-six, and of the Independence of the United States of America the two hundredth.

GERALD R. FORD

NOTES

PREFACE

1. Kazuo Miyamoto, *Hawaii: End of the Rainbow.*

2. Michi Weglyn, *Years of Infamy: The Untold Story of America's Concentration Camps,* 6.

3. Dr. Eugene Rostow, quoted in Weglyn, *Years of Infamy,* 53.

4. For accounts of Washington State's Japanese American community, see David Takami, *Divided Destiny: A History of Japanese Americans in Seattle;* and Gail Nomura, "Washington's Asian / Pacific American Communities." For Japanese Americans and World War II, see Weglyn, *Years of Infamy;* Frank Chuman, *The Bamboo People: The Law and Japanese-Americans;* and United States Commission on Wartime Relocation and Internment of Civilians, *Personal Justice Denied: Report of the Commission on Wartime Relocation and Internment of Civilians.*

1 / AWAKENING

1. Michi Weglyn, *Years of Infamy: The Untold Story of America's Concentration Camps.*

2. The term *Nikkei* refers to all persons of Japanese ancestry, wherever they may live.

3. Conversation between Mike Nakata and Henry Miyatake related by Miyatake, personal interview, May 19, 1997; verified by Nakata, personal interview, Oct. 23, 1997.

4. Charles Z. Smith, personal interview, Nov. 15, 1997.

5. Tomio Moriguchi, personal interviews with Chuck Kato and the author, Apr. 1997.

6. "An Interview with Henry Miyatake."

7. Executive Order 9066, signed by President Roosevelt on Feb. 19, 1942, "gave to

the Secretary of War, and the military commanders to whom he delegated authority, the power to exclude any and all persons, citizens and aliens, from designated areas in order to provide security against sabotage, espionage and fifth column activity"; see United States Commission on Wartime Relocation and Internment of Civilians, *Personal Justice Denied: Report of the Commission on Wartime Relocation and Internment of Civilians,* 2. Whereas E.O. 9066 gave military commanders the power to exclude individuals, "Public Law 503 made it a federal offense to violate any and all restrictions issued by a military commander in a 'military area'" and "provided for enforcement in the federal courts." P.L. 503 passed both houses of Congress unanimously on March 19, 1942, and was signed by the president on March 21 (Weglyn, *Years of Infamy,* 72).

8. Internees could leave camp to go to school, or to work outside the designated military zones, as long as they did not return to their former homes. Some left as soon as they could. Some were drafted out. Some were thrown in prison; the reasons varied.

9. Henry Miyatake, personal interview, Feb. 23, 1998.

10. Ibid.

11. In *ex parte Milligan* (1866), the Supreme Court invalidated an Indiana citizen's conviction by a military court on charges of aiding Confederate rebels and inciting insurrection, ruling that civilians may not be tried by military tribunals as long as civilian courts are open.

12. Morris Cohen, Robert Berring, and Kent Olsen, *How to Find the Law.*

13. Jacobus tenBroek, Edward Barnhart, and Floyd Matson, *Prejudice, War, and the Constitution.*

14. Henry Miyatake, personal interview, May 19, 1997.

15. Professor Arval Morris, in a phone conversation with the author on July 18, 1999, verified Miyatake's account of the legal advice he offered Miyatake.

16. Minoru Masuda, *Pride and Shame* grant proposal to the National Endowment for the Humanities, Oct. 22, 1970.

17. Also involved were Larry Matsuda, June Shimokawa, Kay Hashimoto, and Elaine Nakai (*Pride and Shame* Committee meeting notes, May 25, 1971).

18. Fujii claimed no ownership over the logo and later said, "It was for everyone to use"; Frank Fujii, personal interview, Apr. 1997.

19. Minoru Masuda, *Pride and Shame* grant report to the National Endowment for the Humanities, Oct. 28, 1975. (In 1977, Western Washington State College was renamed Western Washington State University.)

20. Calvin Takagi, personal interview, Sept. 1997.

21. Ken Nakano, personal interview, Aug. 16, 1999.

22. Chuck Kato, personal interview, undated.

2 / ROADBLOCKS

1. Shosuke Sasaki, interviewed by Frank Abe, The Densho Project, May 18, 1997.

2. Ken Nakano, on working with the Seattle Evacuation Redress Committee; personal interview, Aug. 16, 1999.

3. Mike Nakata, personal interview, Oct. 23, 1997.

4. Shosuke Sasaki, interviewed by Frank Abe.

5. Mike Nakata, personal interview.

6. Shosuke Sasaki, interviewed by Frank Abe.

7. See n. 7, chap. 1.

8. Because of the resistance to redress being expressed by some in the Japanese community, Miyatake added a provision allowing those who did not wish to receive redress to choose not to participate in the redress checkoff plan. This provision would later be challenged by William Hohri (see n. 10) and the National Council for Japanese American Redress, who felt it was questionable constitutionally (see n. 17, chap. 4).

9. Mike Nakata, personal interview.

10. The activist was William Hohri, a member of the Redress Committee of the Chicago JACL chapter and author of *Repairing America*. The advantages of Miyatake's plan were explained to Hohri by Shosuke Sasaki in a letter dated Aug. 6, 1979, in which Sasaki mentioned a fact that Miyatake had already figured out: "The Japanese Americans are the only minority which had a per capita income high enough to make this kind of bootstrap plan practical."

11. Ben Nakagawa, letter to the author, Jan. 19, 1999. Others, such as William Hohri, would later reject Miyatake's funding plan for the same reason.

12. The resolution had been passed at the Pacific Northwest District Council (PNWDC) meeting of November 24, 1973 (meeting minutes, dated Nov. 25, 1973, courtesy of Homer and Miyuki Yasui collection, Portland).

13. Yasuko Takezawa, *Breaking the Silence: Redress and Japanese American Ethnicity*, 35–36: "At the 1970 national JACL convention in Chicago, Edison Uno, a lecturer at San Francisco State University, introduced a resolution calling for redress for internment. He proposed that the JACL petition the American government to admit its mistake in denying the civil and constitutional rights of Japanese Americans during the war. . . . Although he believed that redress should include acknowledgment of legal liability, he proposed no concrete plan at that point."

14. The PNWDC generally supported reparations but never formally approved any reparations plan. Ed Yamamoto of the Columbia Basin chapter had attempted to get his plan approved by the PNWDC at the meetings of Oct. 8, 1972, July 15, 1973, and

Sept. 29, 1974. The Columbia Basin plan, as it came to be known, requested (in its 1974 version) that the United States "take any and all steps necessary to provide for the payment of Reparations in the amount of $1,614,000,000." The plan called for the reparations to be held in two equal trust foundations, one for "educational and such other purposes for the betterment of the life and lot of Japanese Americans and other Asian American minorities within the United States," and the other for establishing a public relations organization for U.S.–Japanese cultural exchange. At the 1972 and 1974 meetings, the PNWDC referred the plan for study to Edison Uno and others at the national JACL; the 1973 PNWDC meeting recommended that "all residents of the Western Defense Command be given consideration and included in the final decisions about reparations" (PNWDC minutes for the meetings cited).

15. PNWDC meeting minutes, Sept. 29, 1974.

16. Ibid.

17. Ibid.

18. Later, Seattle Betsuin contributed money for the "Appeal for Action" tapes (see the section of this chapter titled "1975: 'The Appeal for Action'") and joined the Community Committee on Redress / Reparations in 1980 (see chap. 5).

19. Kaz Oshiki, personal communication, May 12, 1998.

20. Kaz Oshiki, memo to PEC members, Jan. 16, 1976: 2.

21. Shosuke Sasaki, Mike Nakata, and Henry Miyatake, "An Appeal for Action to Obtain Redress for the World War II Evacuation and Imprisonment of Japanese Americans."

22. Charles Z. Smith, letter to Henry Miyatake, Jan. 16, 1976.

23. The Nikkei newspapers were *Rafu Shimpo, Hokubei Mainichi, Nichibei Times,* and *New York Nichibei.*

24. Statistics taken from tallied surveys as reported by SERC in a letter to JACL chapter presidents, May 31, 1976.

25. S. I. Hayakawa, "Radical Chic among the Japanese," A12.

26. Shosuke Sasaki, "Hayakawa Discredits Only Himself," A13.

27. Paul Isaki, "Washington Governor Set Motion for President Ford's Revocation of E.O. 9066," 1.

28. Wayne Horiuchi, confidential memo to the national JACL board, undated.

29. Bill Hosokawa, *JACL in Quest of Justice: The History of the Japanese American Citizens League,* 340.

30. President Gerald Ford, "An American Promise," Feb. 19, 1976.

31. Jim Tsujimura, personal communication, Nov. 5, 1998.

32. Mike Masaoka, "Reparations for Evacuees Urged on Individual Basis, May Rally JACL Nationally," D-1.

33. See n. 14.

34. According to Ken Nakano's notes, Henry Miyatake, Shosuke Sasaki, Chuck Kato, Ken Nakano, and Tomio Moriguchi met with Mike Masaoka and Edison Uno, but "Mike [Masaoka] didn't agree with our plan fully that time."

35. "National Council Narrative—2nd Day Highlights: Hibakusha, Reparations," 3; minutes of national JACL convention, Sacramento, Calif., June 21–26, 1976.

36. "National Council Narrative—2nd Day Highlights," 1.

37. The National JACL Reparations Committee succeeded Ed Yamamoto's REPACAMP. A national redress meeting, JACL's first, was convened in Portland May 8–9, 1976, with district redress representatives in attendance. The purpose of the redress committee was to consider the redress proposals on the table.

38. For further discussion of JACL's role in the forced evacuation, see Weglyn, *Years of Infamy*; Hohri, *Repairing America*; Hosokawa, JACL in Quest of Justice; and Deborah K. Lim, *Research Report Prepared for Presidential Select Committee on JACL Resolution #7* (also known as *The Lim Report*).

39. Jim Tsujimura's notes.

40. William Hohri, *Repairing America,* 43: Iva Toguri was "accused, tried and convicted of treason and served a ten-year sentence for being 'Tokyo Rose.' The evidence clearly pointed to a gross miscarriage of justice, which had been prompted by the news media's vindictive hatred of Japan. The effort for a pardon was nationwide, led by a committee of the JACL." In 1977, after a two-year campaign, Toguri received a presidential pardon. See also Frank Chuman, *Bamboo People,* 290–95.

41. As Uyeda now recalls, Ed Yamamoto phoned him three times before he assented. According to Jim Tsujimura and others, however, it was Tsujimura who asked Uyeda to chair the committee. Both Cherry Kinoshita and John Tateishi recall that Uyeda at the time said Tsujimura had asked him to chair the committee.

42. Clifford Uyeda, personal communication, Sept. 7, 1998.

43. Clifford Uyeda, "Why Reparation?" All of Uyeda's articles appeared weekly in the *Pacific Citizen* between Oct. 28, 1977, and July 21, 1978.

44. Ibid., 1.

45. The term *reparations* had been eliciting negative comments, according to Clifford Uyeda, "A Change to 'Redress,'" (47): "Aside from its strictly dictionary definition, there is a strong emotional reaction attached to the term 'reparation.' It is war related, and is usually associated with the payment forced upon the defeated by the victor. . . . In the national campaign we will use such terms as redress and restitution. The committee will be the JACL National Committee for Redress. It is to be noted that 'redress' is the term that has been used by the Seattle group for many years." Miyatake's comment: "The term redress was used from October 1975, after the Tri-

District Council meeting in Anaheim, California"; former Nixon aide John Dean, speaking at that meeting, had suggested the term.

46. Clifford Uyeda, personal communication, Aug. 28, 1998.

47. Bill Hosokawa, JACL in Quest of Justice, 348.

48. Ibid., 347. Also, according to Clifford Uyeda, Hayakawa was invited to speak by the host Salt Lake City chapter. National JACL had originally invited Sen. Spark Matsunaga of Hawaii, who, having already accepted, had to be "disinvited."

49. The participants in the September 1978 meeting of the National Committee for Redress were John Tateishi (chair), Henry Miyatake, Raymond Okamura, Phil Shigekuni, and Minoru Yasui, along with subcommittee chairs Ellen Endo (media) and Ron Mamiya (legislation); Clifford Uyeda (national president); Jim Tsujimura (national vice president); Frank Chin (present at the invitation of the chair); and Paula Mitsunaga (recording secretary). Also present was Ben Takeshita, the Northern California / Western Nevada District Council Reparations Committee chair. Meeting minutes of the National Committee for Redress courtesy of Ron Mamiya and the Frank Abe collection.

50. Meeting minutes of the National Committee for Redress, Sept. 9, 1978.

51. Ibid.

52. In the Native Alaskan Land Claims Settlement Act of 1971, all Native Alaskan land claims to almost all of Alaska were dropped in exchange for approximately one-ninth of the state's land plus $962.5 million in compensation.

53. Meeting minutes of the National Committee for Redress, Sept. 9, 1978.

54. John Tateishi, letter to congressional members, Sept. 26, 1978.

55. Daniel Inouye, letter to Clifford Uyeda, Sept. 13, 1978.

56. John Tateishi, memo to JACL chapter presidents, Feb. 8, 1979, reporting on the meeting between JACL representatives and Nikkei members of the U.S. Senate and House of Representatives held on Feb. 1, 1979, in Washington, D.C. Uyeda has said that the memo is incorrect, and that the meeting was actually held on Jan. 30.

3 / REMEMBRANCE

1. Remarks made at the first Day of Remembrance, Puyallup Fairgrounds, Puyallup, Wash., Nov. 25, 1978.

2. Frank Abe, personal communication, Oct. 23, 1997.

3. As Chin further explained (personal interview, Nov. 1, 1997), "JA art is only going to be taken as seriously as JA history. Without [redress], . . . JAs won't have respect for themselves. How can people who have no respect for themselves produce art?"

4. Ibid.

5. Frank Abe, personal communication. Lillian Baker and her group, Americans for Historical Accuracy, vigorously argued in every public arena they could that there had been nothing wrong with the camps, and that they had merely been "relocation centers": "To listen to her was to relive the times of World War II" (Hohri, *Repairing America*, 96). Despite Baker's vigilance, the amateur historian (as she often called herself) was rarely taken seriously by any institutional body.

6. Frank Chin, "Days of Remembrance."

7. Mike Lowry, personal interview, July 22, 1997.

8. Henry Miyatake, personal interview, May 19, 1997.

9. Aki Kurose, personal interview, Feb. 26, 1998.

10. Frank Chin, personal interview, Nov. 1, 1997; Frank Abe, personal communication, Nov. 29, 1999.

11. Chin, "Days of Remembrance."

12. Much of the narrative in this section is based on my interview with Frank Chin.

13. Will Lawson, "Internment: A Reminder of Injustice in Wartime," A9.

14. Cherry Kinoshita, interviewed by Tracy Lai and Becky Fukuda, The Densho Project, Sept. 26, 1997.

15. Chin, "Days of Remembrance."

16. David Horsey, "Japanese Don't Forget Internment," 1.

17. Ibid.

18. Frank Abe, personal interview, Oct. 12, 1997.

19. The reasons for the cancellation are not entirely clear. Frank Chin says that Ellen Endo, who in addition to serving as media chair of the JACL National Committee for Redress was a vice president for standards and ethics at ABC, nixed the *20/20* segment because the Day of Remembrance was not a JACL affair, and because some ABC executives took issue with the description of the camps as "concentration camps."

20. John Tateishi, letter to Ron Mamiya, Nov. 27, 1978. Ron Mamiya's papers. See also n. 19.

21. "Hayakawa Vows to Filibuster," 3, 12.

22. Ibid., 1, 3.

23. Karen Seriguchi, former president and managing director of the Asian American Theater Workshop, had been working on redress at the national JACL office when Frank Chin convinced her to move to Seattle, because that was "where the action was" regarding redress; Karen Seriguchi, interview questionnaire from Yasuko Takezawa, 1988, unpublished, courtesy of Karen Seriguchi.

24. Katsuyoshi Nishimura, unpublished document, March 14, 1979.

25. Walter M. Weglyn, letter to the editor, *Pacific Citizen*, July 13, 1979, 4. Frank Abe collection.

26. Mia Hayashida, undated letter to the DOR committee, "Dear David Ishii" file; courtesy of Frank Abe.

27. Days of Remembrance Steering Committee, "Open Letter to Senator Hayakawa."

4 / CIRCUMVENTION

1. John Tateishi, memo to JACL Chapter Presidents, Dec. 15, 1978.

2. Unless otherwise noted, information and quotes in this chapter come from Tateishi's Feb. 8, 1979, report to JACL chapter presidents.

3. Tateishi's report (see n. 2) dates this meeting as Feb. 1; Clifford Uyeda has attested that the meeting with the Nikkei congressional delegation was actually on Jan. 30. Also at the meeting were Clifford Uyeda, JACL national president; Karl Nobuyuki, JACL national director; Ron Ikejiri, JACL Washington representative; John Tateishi, chair of the JACL National Committee for Redress; and Ron Mamiya, a member of the JACL National Committee for Redress. Meeting minutes, Feb. 1, 1979.

4. Dwight Chuman, "JACL Committee Finalizes Redress Legislation Proposal," 1.

5. Ron Mamiya, letter to John Tateishi, Clifford Uyeda, and Jim Tsujimura, March 12, 1979.

6. Ibid.

7. John Tateishi, letter to Ron Mamiya, March 19, 1979.

8. Mich Matsudaira, letter to John Tateishi, March 24, 1979.

9. John Tateishi, letter to Henry Miyatake, Apr. 30, 1979.

10. Clifford Uyeda, letter to Mich Matsudaira, July 3, 1979.

11. Seattle Chapter JACL, chapter ballot form; courtesy of Mich Matsudaira.

12. Dwight Chuman, "Inouye, Matsunaga, Hayakawa Propose 'Study' on Internment," 1.

13. Leslie T. Hatamiya, *Righting a Wrong*, xix.

14. William Hohri, *Repairing America*, 47–50.

15. Ibid., 50.

16. Ibid.

17. Ibid. Hohri also objected to the requirement for victims to assign their taxes to the redress fund: "Victims should not have to do any such thing to receive their just due."

18. Frank Abe, "Pride and Shame," 13.

19. Ibid.

20. Mike Lowry, interviewed by Ruthann Kurose, July 22, 1997.

21. Ibid.

22. Hatamiya, *Righting a Wrong.*

23. Hohri, *Repairing America,* 71–78. According to Hohri and Miyatake, the Nisei Lobby consisted only of Mike Masaoka.

24. Yasuko Takezawa, *Breaking the Silence: Redress and Japanese American Ethnicity,* 47.

25. United States Commission on Wartime Relocation and Internment of Civilians, *Personal Justice Denied,* 1.

5 / TESTIMONY

1. Frank Abe at Seattle hearings of the Commission on Wartime Relocation and Internment of Civilians (CWRIC), cited in William Hohri, *Repairing America,* 137.

2. Emi Somekawa, written testimony, Seattle CWRIC hearings, Sept. 10, 1981; courtesy of Frank Abe.

3. Ken Nakano, personal interview, Aug. 16, 1999.

4. Cherry Kinoshita, interviewed by Tracy Lai and Becky Fukuda, The Densho Project, Sept. 26, 1997.

5. Ibid.

6. Ibid.

7. Ibid.

8. According to Cherry Kinoshita, representatives to CCRR included Amy Doi, Mark Fugami, Akio Hoshino, Kibo Inouye, Kaz Ishimitsu, Harry Kadoshima, John Kanda, Chuck Kato, Joe Kosai, Ken Nakano, Joe Nakatsu, Hiro Nishimura, Richard Nishioka, Sam Shoji, Theresa Takayoshi, Massie Tomita, and Harvey Watanabe.

9. Meeting minutes, redress committee of Seattle Chapter JACL, Aug. 15, 1980.

10. Chuck Kato, answer to questionnaire prepared for a conference titled "The Voices of Japanese American Redress," held at the University of California at Los Angeles, Sept. 11, 1997; courtesy of Chuck Kato. It should be noted that in October 1980 the Seattle redress movement had received a huge boost: Karen Seriguchi was hired as secretary of the JACL Pacific Northwest District (later she would be named director). In January of that year, she and Frank Abe had organized "Contemporary Perspectives on the Internment," a one-day conference in Seattle on redress issues. As she had done with the open letter to S. I. Hayakawa (see chap. 3), Seriguchi attracted generous media coverage of the conference, which drew a crowd of more than 400 people. The coverage included a feature in the Sunday *Seattle Times* and spots on radio and nightly television news programs. Similar conferences, held in Tacoma and Spokane, also received much media attention. Seriguchi's new job, a half-time position, represented a substantial commitment of time and energy, but she continued

to devote the majority of her waking hours to preparing the community for the commission hearings.

11. Community Committee on Redress / Reparations, letter to the Japanese American community, Feb. 1, 1981.

12. Carey Quan Gelernter, "Most World War II Internees Seek Redress, Survey Shows," C1.

13. Community Committee on Redress / Reparations, "Summary of Activities through Apr. 15, 1981," 2.

14. Community Committee on Redress / Reparations, "Summary of Activities," 1.

15. Ibid.

16. Ibid.

17. Ibid.

18. Ibid.

19. Ibid.

20. Ruth Pumphrey, "Japanese Seek Internment Redress," F1.

21. Carey Quan Gelernter, "Japanese-Americans Practice Hearings," C1.

22. Ibid.

23. Cherry Kinoshita, interview with Tracy Lai and Becky Fukuda. In the minutes for the CCRR meeting of Aug. 18, 1981, Kato and Theresa Takayoshi, who had attended the Los Angeles hearings, reported that the commissioners had seemed most impressed by the expert testimony, particularly from psychologists and anthropologists. Most witnesses in Los Angeles had ended their testimonies with appeals for money, and Kinoshita, reporting on the hearings in San Francisco, said that the witnesses there had also generally requested money ($25,000 minimum). The audience's cheering and booing in Los Angeles had brought about the suggestion that an effort be made to control the crowd in Seattle so as to allow a dignified hearing. The length of the testimonies had also been an issue in Los Angeles and San Francisco.

24. Gerald Sato, "L.A. Nikkei Not Fulfilling Leadership Role in Redress Movement," 1.

25. Gerald Sato, "Looking Back at the Seattle Hearings: Commissioners Come Alive, Audience Quiets," 1.

26. Hohri, *Repairing America*, 130.

27. Emi Somekawa, National Archives, RG 220, Records of Temporary Committees, Commissions, and Boards, Series CWRIC, 1981 Seattle, Washington, Hearings. Somekawa's testimony about this incident is reproduced in more detail in John Tateishi, *And Justice for All: An Oral History of the Japanese American Detention Camps*, 149:

One day her husband came and said that he just couldn't stand watching breathing, a very labored type of breathing, day after day. Would we please take her out of her misery. . . . The doctor said we had nothing here to offer her, and if that's the wishes of the family, then he'll go along with it. And so then we talked about it and I think it was the next day the husband came back again with his family. This was her fifth pregnancy. He had four children, and they were all still little. The first one might have been in grammar school, but not much older. They all came. He had made his decision; this was what he was going to do.

So he talked to the doctor again, who told me to fix up a fourth of morphine. So I was there. There was a teaspoon there with some water in it, and the father told each child to give the mother a sip of water, and after the last child gave the sip of water, the father did the same thing, and then he was ready for the morphine. That was it. That was it. . . . You know, I feel this might have been a legitimate thing to do for a woman in that condition. But I feel that if we were not in camp, that there might have been some other treatment.

28. See Hohri, *Repairing America*.

29. United States Commission on Wartime Relocation and Internment of Civilians, *Personal Justice Denied*, 8.

30. Ibid., 10.

31. Angus Macbeth, special counsel to CWRIC, reported this information as a participant in the CWRIC panel at "The Voices of Japanese American Redress" (see n. 10).

32. United States Commission on Wartime Relocation and Internment of Civilians, *Personal Justice Denied*, 27–28.

6 / GESTURES

1. "Overdue Apology," A14.

2. Cherry Kinoshita, interviewed by Tracy Lai and Becky Fukuda, The Densho Project, Sept. 26, 1997.

3. Ibid.

4. Ron Sims, personal interview, Aug. 13, 1997.

5. Ibid.

6. Ibid.

7. Ibid.

8. Ibid.

9. Ibid.

10. Ibid.

11. Cherry Kinoshita, "Compensation Bill for Salary Losses of Japanese American Employees of the State of Washington." Tomo-no-kai (a community service organization), the Washington Commission on Asian American Affairs (a governor's advisory board), and Chizu Omori joined the nucleus of organizations that stayed with the redress effort from the late seventies through the nineties. For a full list of CCRR / WCR representatives, see n. 8, chap. 5.

12. Cherry Kinoshita, letter to state legislators, undated; courtesy of Cherry Kinoshita.

13. Chuck Kato, personal interview, Oct. 20, 1999.

14. Cherry Kinoshita, letter to JACL Pacific Northwest District chapter presidents, Jan. 14, 1983.

15. George Fleming, interviewed by the author and Cherry Kinoshita, May 18, 1998.

16. A plaque in the Seattle JACL office lists the names of those who were instrumental in the lobbying effort: George Fukano, Aya Hurd, Mae Ishihara, Chuck Kato, Wayne Kimura, Frank Kinomoto, Cherry Kinoshita, Kara Kondo, Bill Kunitsugu, Mitzi Kunitsugu, Aki Kurose, Junelow Kurose, Kibo Inouye, Mako Nakagawa, Ken Nakano, Joe Nakatsu, Kenko Nogaki, Chiz Omori, Tom Scott, Karen Seriguchi, Tom Shigio, Emi Somekawa, Theresa Takayoshi, Tom Takemura, Grace Tatsumi, Masako Tomita, Jane Yambe, and Denny Yasuhara.

17. Duane Kaiser, address to the Washington House of Representatives, May 6, 1983.

18. Ray Isaacson, address to the Washington House of Representatives, May 6, 1983.

19. Sentiment expressed to Gov. Gary Locke, related in personal interview with the governor, Feb. 27, 1998.

20. Art Wang, address to the Washington House of Representatives, May 6, 1983.

21. Ron Sims, personal interview.

22. Ibid.

23. Ruth Woo, personal interview, Apr. 23, 1998.

24. Ron Sims, personal interview.

25. George Fleming, quoted in Louis Fiset, "Redress for Nisei Public Employees in Washington State after World War II," 27.

26. Gov. Gary Locke, address to the Washington House of Representatives, May 6, 1983.

27. Cherry Kinoshita's notes.

28. In his May 6 address to the House, Locke reported that other organizations

supporting the state redress bill included the AFL–CIO, the Asian Pacific Women's Caucus, the Church Council of Greater Seattle, the Greater Seattle Chapter of the American Jewish Committee, the Washington Association of Churches, the Washington Commission on Asian American Affairs, the Washington Federation of State Employees, and the Washington State Catholic Conference.

29. Ron Sims, personal interview.

30. United States Commission on Wartime Relocation and Internment of Civilians, *Personal Justice Denied*, 461.

31. Miye Ishihara, testimony to the Washington State Legislature, Feb. 1, 1983.

32. Lila Fujimoto, "Sculptor George Tsutakawa, on the Puyallup Memorial Controversy," 10.

33. Ibid.

34. Roger Shimizu, personal communication, June 1998.

35. This committee was formed to raise funds for the memorial and for the dedication and unveiling ceremonies. Its members were Emi Somekawa, Henry Miyatake, Tom Shigio, Ken Nakano, Mako Nakagawa, Chuck Kato, Ken Okuma, Kaz Ishimitsu, Kazzie Katayama, Akio Hoshino, David Hoekendorf, Karen Seriguchi, Massie Tomita, Saki Shimizu, and Roger Shimizu.

36. Fujimoto, "Sculptor George Tsutakawa, on the Puyallup Memorial Controversy," 10.

37. Carlton Smith, "Memorial Dedicated to Japanese-Americans," B14.

38. Sumiko Kuriyama, testimony before Seattle City Council, Feb. 15, 1984.

39. Dolores Sibonga, memo to Susan Pavlou, March 28, 1983.

40. Susan Pavlou, memo to Dolores Sibonga, Apr. 1, 1983.

41. Peter Tormey, "Sibonga Seeks to Redress Interned Japanese," 7.

42. Sumiko Kuriyama, testimony before Seattle City Council.

43. City of Seattle, Ordinance 11571, March 6, 1984.

44. Sumiko Haji, Ruth Kazama, and Thomas Kobayashi received redress from the City of Seattle. Satoshi Shiota was never located, and Don Kazama did not qualify because he had left for military service in February 1942. See Fiset, "Redress for Nisei Public Employees," 26, 31*n*.42.

45. May Daty Namba, testimony before Seattle School Board, Apr. 11, 1984.

46. Quoted in "Japanese Girls Resign Positions in City Schools." WCR first learned of the former school district clerks from this news story, included in a collection of clippings gathered by Yoriko Watanabe Sasaki, Shosuke Sasaki's wife (see n. 48).

47. Kinoshita, "Compensation Bill for Salary Losses," journal attachment.

48. Well after her death, Yoriko Watanabe Sasaki's brother, James Watanabe, discovered her extensive collection of materials about Japanese Americans from late

1941 up to the incarceration. Watanabe had the materials printed and bound in the fall of 1982.

49. The 27 Japanese American clerks had composed one-fourth of the district's clerical support personnel. In 1942, a Seattle School District official explained the reason for such a large proportion of Japanese American clerks by stating that the "good white help had left the District for higher-paying war industry employment." War-industry jobs were off limits to Japanese Americans, unions were vigorously "restricted," and employment opportunities were very limited for those who were not white. (One of the former clerks, May Ota, had earned a college degree and a teaching certificate, but, knowing that because of her ethnicity she would not be hired by any school district as a certified teacher, she accepted the position of clerk with the Seattle schools.) These women were also underpaid by the district, earning seven and a half cents below the minimum wage at the time, a fact that they were not aware of until the mid-1980s.

50. T. J. Vassar, personal interview, May 15, 1998.

51. "School Mothers Protest Japanese Office Girls"; article courtesy of Cherry Kinoshita.

52. Quotations taken from articles in Cherry Kinoshita's papers, courtesy of Cherry Kinoshita.

53. Anona Hales, undated and unpaginated photocopy of letter to the editor of the *Seattle Post-Intelligencer*; courtesy of Cherry Kinoshita.

54. Charlotte Drysdale, undated and unpaginated photocopy of letter to the editor of the *Seattle Post-Intelligencer*; courtesy of Cherry Kinoshita.

55. Fiset, "Redress for Nisei Public Employees," 21–31.

56. Misao Sakamoto, "Statement of Misao Sakamoto," Aug. 16, 1983; courtesy of Cherry Kinoshita.

57. May Ota Higa, letter to Cherry Kinoshita, July 21, 1983; emphasis added.

58. Letter to Seattle School Board; courtesy of Cherry Kinoshita.

59. According to the minutes of the Seattle School Board meeting of Feb. 27, 1942, the group of citizens who spoke out included the Reverends Jenson, Shorter, and Binders, "Mesdames Hale, McRae and Morris," Ray Roberts, and "Miss Libbee," a teacher (Seattle School Board, record 38, 228). The University of Washington student petition is cited in "Resignation of Japanese OK'd."

60. Quoted in "Japanese Girls Resign Positions in City Schools."

61. Letters of support also came from the American Civil Liberties Union, the Asian / Pacific Women's Caucus, the Anti-Defamation League of B'nai B'rith, the Center for Career Alternatives, the Samoan Polynesian Community, the Seattle Human Rights Commission, and the Washington State Commission on Asian American Affairs.

62. All quotations from testimony courtesy of Cherry Kinoshita.

63. See n. 5, chap. 3.

64. James K. Pharris, letter to Cherry Kinoshita, Aug. 9, 1985; courtesy of Cherry Kinoshita.

65. Co-sponsors of H.B. 1415 included Katie Allen, Jennifer Belcher, Louise Miller, Ken Jacobsen, Eugene Lux, Janice Niemi, Eugene Prince, Jay Vander Stoep, and Jolene Unsoeld; State of Washington 49th Legislature, H.B. 1415, 1986, 1. Co-sponsors of S.B. 3369 included Arlie DeJarnatt, George Fleming, Myron Kreider, and Phil Talmadge; State of Washington 49th Legislature, S.B. 3369, 1986, 1.

66. State of Washington 49th Legislature, Final Passage H.B. 1415, third reading, Feb. 15, 1986.

67. Senate vote on H.B. 1415: 45 yeas, 1 nay, 2 absent, 1 excused. State of Washington 49th Legislature, Final Passage H.B. 1415, roll call, March 6, 1986.

7 / DETERMINATION

1. Document courtesy of Cherry Kinoshita.

2. Chuck Kato, personal interview, Sept. 22, 1997.

3. A draft dated Apr. 19, 1983, also included as "eligible individuals" all who had faced expulsion or incarceration because of governmental acts during World War II: Latin Americans of Japanese ancestry, Aleuts, Germans, and Italians; document courtesy of Ruthann Kurose. Although it was called the World War II Japanese American Civil Rights Violations Act, the proposed bill described itself as "a Bill to provide for payments to certain legal residents or citizens of the United States of Japanese, Aleut, or other ancestry who were interned, detained, or forcibly relocated by the United States during World War II." The proposal also defined an eligible individual as

> (1) any individual of Japanese or Alaskan Aleut ancestry enrolled on the records of the United States government during the period beginning on Dec. 7, 1941, and ending on Sept. 30, 1952, as being in a prohibited military zone, or (2) *any individual of other racial and ancestral background* who was confined, held in custody, or otherwise deprived of liberty or property during the period as a result of Executive Order Numbered 9066 (issued Feb. 19, 1942), or the Act entitled "An Act to provide a penalty for violation of restrictions or orders with respect to persons entering, remaining in, leaving, or committing any act in military areas or zones" and approved March 21, 1942 (56 Stat. 173), or as a result of any other Executive Order [or] Presidential proclamation [emphasis added].

4. Rep. Tom Foley, letter to Cherry Kinoshita, Aug. 4, 1983.

5. John Tateishi, memo to JACL chapter presidents and chapter redress representatives, Oct. 10, 1983.

6. Rod Chandler, letter to Ken (Akira) Nakano, June 22, 1984.

7. Al Swift, letter to Mayme (Semba) Nishimura, June 6, 1984.

8. Calvin Naito, "Against All Odds: The Japanese Americans' Campaign for Redress," 14.

9. Cherry Kinoshita, letter to John Miller, Nov. 7, 1984.

10. Sid Morrison, letter to Karen Seriguchi, June 2, 1983.

11. Cherry Kinoshita, "Reflections on the JACL Lobbying Experience," E5.

12. Brock Adams, letter to Seattle Redress Project, May 1, 1998.

13. Calvin Naito, "Against All Odds," 20.

14. The *coram nobis* cases involved the 1980s attempt to reverse the World War II–era convictions of Fred Korematsu, Gordon Hirabayashi, and Minoru Yasui, three Japanese Americans who challenged the constitutionality of E.O. 9066 and P.L. 503. The Supreme Court had upheld their convictions and the constitutionality of the laws on the basis of military necessity. In the early 1980s, CWRIC researcher Aiko Yoshinaga Herzig and attorney Peter Irons discovered documents in the National Archives verifying that the government had withheld information showing that there had been no military necessity for the forcible removal of Japanese Americans from the West Coast. Included in the documents were statements by the Federal Communications Commission, the Federal Bureau of Investigation, and the Office of Naval Intelligence indicating no evidence of espionage, disloyalty, or fifth-column activity on the part of Japanese Americans. The documents also verified that "the federal government not only was aware of the lack of military necessity but also intentionally suppressed this awareness and presented statements to the Supreme Court that it knew to be false"; see Maki, Kitano, and Berthold, *Achieving the Impossible Dream: How Japanese Americans Obtained Redress,* 129. Although the *coram nobis* cases did not reach the United States Supreme Court for a ruling on the constitutionality of the laws, all three convictions were vacated. For a short summary of the cases, see Maki, Kitano, and Berthold, *Achieving the Impossible Dream,* 128–136. For a more detailed account, see Peter Irons, *Justice at War: The Story of the Japanese American Internment Cases.*

15. Ben Nakagawa, personal interview, Nov. 18, 1997.

16. Ken Nakano's notes.

17. Rep. Don Bonker, letter to Tim Otani, JACL Pacific Northwest District, June 12, 1985.

18. Rep. Don Bonker, letter to Cherry Kinoshita / Washington Coalition on Redress, May 12, 1986.

19. Kinoshita, "Reflections on the JACL Lobbying Experience," E5.

20. Rep. Don Bonker, letter to Cherry Kinoshita, JACL Legislative Education Committee, Sept. 2, 1987.

21. Kinoshita, "Reflections on the JACL Lobbying Experience," E5.

22. Rep. Al Swift, letter to the Seattle Redress Project, May 14, 1998.

23. Kinoshita, "Reflections on the JACL Lobbying Experience," E5.

24. Ibid.

25. Numerous visits with Rep. Norm Dicks by Joe Kosai and Puyallup JACLers had also been successful.

26. The Office of Redress Administration (ORA) was created by the Civil Liberties Act to search for eligible recipients and distribute redress funds to them. The ORA was also responsible for initially determining eligibility, although the courts had final say in individual cases on appeal.

27. Robert Shimabukuro, "Centenarians Receive Redress Checks," 1–2.

8 / ARRIVAL

1. Mike Lowry, personal interview, July 22, 1997.

2. Henry Miyatake was invited but was unable to attend the signing. Chuck Kato was also invited but did not attend. As for Lowry's non-appearance, a Republican representative from San Diego, William Lowery, is in the photo, having mistakenly been invited to the signing instead of Lowry. The press release that accompanies the photo identifies Lowery as "Bill Lowery (R-Wash)." As one WCR member indignantly scoffed, "[Lowery] didn't even vote for the bill. How could he even show up?"

3. Clifford Uyeda, personal communication, Aug. 28, 1998.

4. Information about attendance at the celebration comes from Yasuko Takezawa, *Breaking the Silence: Redress and Japanese American Ethnicity,* 56–57. Frank Chin's comments were made in a telephone interview, Nov. 1, 1977.

5. Karen Seriguchi, personal communication, Oct. 22, 1999.

6. Frank Chin, "How Shall Injustice Be Served?" 15.

7. Miyatake sensed that it was not just Boeing managers and the greater American citizenry who were not paying Issei and Nisei due respect: the younger Sansei and Yonsei were also questioning the Nisei's quiet acceptance of the wartime expulsion. Miyatake's son's peers were the ones who asked, "Why did it take you so long to do anything?" The high school students of the late 1960s would also become advisers to key officials in the 1980s, and they would play a large part in the success of the city and state redress campaigns.

8. George Fleming, personal interview, May 18, 1998.

9. T. J. Vassar, personal interview, May 15, 1998.

10. Frank Abe, "Pride and Shame," 13.

11. Yasuko Takezawa, *Breaking the Silence,* 59.

12. Cherry Kinoshita, personal communication, Aug. 26, 1998.

13. Henry Miyatake, remarks made at Seattle Redress Committee meeting, May 28, 1998.

14. Rep. Al Swift, letter to the Seattle Redress Project, May 14, 1998.

15. Donna Nagata, reporting on her project to Civil Liberties Public Education Fund conference, June 30, 1998.

16. Miyatake, remarks made at Seattle Redress Committee meeting. Public Law 503 was repealed in Sept. 1976, when "President Ford signed the National Emergencies Act, which terminated certain presidential powers and authorities, as well as section 1383 of Title 18 of the U.S. Code, which was the section of Public Law 503 that specifically provided the criminal penalties for Executive Order 9066"; see Maki, Kitano, and Berthold, *Achieving the Impossible Dream: How Japanese Americans Obtained Redress,* 251.

SOURCES

Abe, Frank. "Pride and Shame." *Seattle Sun,* Dec. 5, 1979, 13.

"An Interview with Henry Miyatake." Newsletter of the National Council for Japanese American Redress, summer 1979.

Chin, Frank. "How Shall Injustice Be Served?" *Seattle Weekly,* Oct. 11–17, 1978, 15.

———. "Days of Remembrance." Unpublished manuscript, 1978–79.

Chuman, Dwight. "JACL Committee Finalizes Redress Legislation Proposal." *Rafu Shimpo,* March 14, 1979 (English section), 1.

———. "Inouye, Matsunaga, Hayakawa Propose 'Study' on Internment." *Rafu Shimpo,* Aug. 2, 1979 (English section), 1.

Chuman, Frank. *The Bamboo People: The Law and Japanese-Americans.* Del Mar, Calif.: Publisher's Inc., 1976.

Cohen, Morris; Berring, Robert; and Olsen, Kent. *How to Find the Law,* 9th ed. St. Paul, Minn.: West, 1989.

Community Committee on Redress / Reparations. "Summary of Activities through Apr. 15, 1981." Seattle, Wash.: Community Committee on Redress / Reparations, 1981.

Days of Remembrance Steering Committee. "Open Letter to Senator Hayakawa." *The Washington Post,* May 9, 1979, A20.

Fiset, Louis. "Redress for Nisei Public Employees in Washington State after World War II." *Pacific Northwest Quarterly,* winter 1996 / 1997, 21–30.

Fujimoto, Lila. "Sculptor George Tsutakawa, on the Puyallup Memorial Controversy." *International Examiner,* Sept. 7, 1983, 10.

Gelernter, Carey Quan. "Japanese-Americans Practice Hearings." *Seattle Times,* May 24, 1981, C1.

———. "Most World War II Internees Seek Redress, Survey Shows." *Seattle Times,* May 25, 1981, C1.

Hatamiya, Leslie T. *Righting a Wrong*. Stanford, Calif.: Stanford University Press, 1993.

Hayakawa, S. I. "Radical Chic among the Japanese." *Seattle Times,* Feb. 3, 1976, A12.

"Hayakawa Vows to Filibuster When Redress Bill Up." Transcript of ABC interview, Jan. 26, 1979, quoted in *Pacific Citizen,* Feb. 9, 1979, 1, 3, 12.

Hohri, William. *Repairing America*. Pullman: Washington State University Press, 1984.

Horsey, David. "Japanese Don't Forget Internment." *Daily Journal American,* Nov. 26, 1998, 1.

Hosokawa, Bill. JACL in Quest of Justice: The History of the Japanese American Citizens League. New York: William Morrow, 1982.

Irons, Peter. *Justice at War: The Story of the Japanese American Internment Cases*. New York: Oxford University Press, 1983.

Isaki, Paul. "Washington Governor Set Motion for President Ford's Revocation of E.O. 9066." *Hokubei Mainichi,* Oct. 5, 1976, 1.

"Japanese Girls Resign Positions in City Schools; 'No Ill Will' Borne." Seattle, Wash.: Untitled volume of documents collected by Yoriko Watanabe Sasaki and compiled by James Watanabe, 1982, unpaginated.

Kinoshita, Cherry. "Compensation Bill for Salary Losses of Japanese American Employees of the State of Washington." Unpublished paper, 1982.

———."Reflections on the JACL Lobbying Experience." *Pacific Citizen,* Dec. 22–29, 1989, E5.

Lawson, Will. "Internment: A Reminder of Injustice in Wartime." *Seattle Post-Intelligencer,* Nov. 26, 1978, A9.

Lim, Deborah K. *Research Report Prepared for Presidential Select Committee on JACL Resolution #7,* 1990. Available at: http://www.resisters.com/study/LimTOC/htm.

Maki, Mitchell; Kitano, Harry; and Berthold, S. Megan. *Achieving the Impossible Dream: How Japanese Americans Obtained Redress*. Urbana and Chicago: University of Illinois Press, 1999.

Masaoka, Mike. "Reparations for Evacuees Urged on Individual Basis, May Rally JACL Nationally." *Pacific Citizen,* Dec. 19–26, 1975, D1, D10–12.

Miyamoto, Kazuo. *Hawaii: End of the Rainbow*. Rutland, Vt.: Charles E. Tuttle, 1964.

Naito, Calvin. "Against All Odds: The Japanese Americans' Campaign for Redress." Case Program, John F. Kennedy School of Government, Harvard University, 1990.

"National Council Narrative—2nd Day Highlights: Hibakusha, Reparations." *Pacific Citizen,* July 16, 1976.

Nomura, Gail. "Washington's Asian / Pacific American Communities." In Sid White and S. E. Solberg, eds., *Peoples of Washington: Perspectives on Cultural Diversity.* Pullman: Washington State University Press, 1989.

"Overdue Apology." *Seattle Post-Intelligencer,* Jan. 20, 1983, A14.

Pumphrey, Ruth. "Japanese Seek Internment Redress." *Seattle Post-Intelligencer,* May 24, 1981, F1.

"Resignation of Japanese OK'd." Seattle, Wash.: Untitled volume of documents collected by Yoriko Watanabe Sasaki and compiled by James Watanabe, 1982, unpaginated.

Sasaki, Shosuke. "Hayakawa Discredits Only Himself." *Seattle Times,* Feb. 11, 1976, A13.

Sasaki, Shosuke, ed.; Nakata, Mike; and Miyatake, Henry. "An Appeal for Action to Obtain Redress for the World War II Evacuation and Imprisonment of Japanese Americans." Seattle, Wash.: Evacuation Redress Committee, Seattle Chapter of the Japanese American Citizens League, 1975.

Sato, Gerald. "L.A. Nikkei Not Fulfilling Leadership Role in Redress Movement." *Rafu Shimpo,* Sept. 23, 1981 (English section), 1.

———. "Looking Back at the Seattle Hearings: Commissioners Come Alive, Audience Quiets." *Rafu Shimpo,* Sept. 22, 1981 (English section), 1.

"School Mothers Protest Japanese Office Girls: Gatewood Group Opens Campaign to Have Nipponese Dismissed." *Seattle Times,* Feb. 24, 1942 (photocopy), page number unknown.

Shimabukuro, Robert. "Centenarians Receive Redress Checks." *International Examiner,* Oct. 17, 1990, 1–2.

Smith, Carlton. "Memorial Dedicated to Japanese-Americans." *Seattle Times,* Aug. 22, 1983, B14.

Takami, David. *Divided Destiny: A History of Japanese Americans in Seattle.* Seattle: Wing Luke Asian Museum / University of Washington Press, 1998.

Takezawa, Yasuko. *Breaking the Silence: Redress and Japanese American Ethnicity.* Ithaca, N.Y.: Cornell University Press, 1995.

Tateishi, John. *And Justice for All: An Oral History of the Japanese American Detention Camps.* New York: Random House, 1984.

tenBroek, Jacobus; Barnhart, Edward; and Matson, Floyd. *Prejudice, War, and the Constitution.* Berkeley: University of California Press, 1954.

Tormey, Peter. "Sibonga Seeks to Redress Interned Japanese." *The Daily* (University of Washington student newspaper), Feb. 15, 1984, 7.

United States Commission on Wartime Relocation and Internment of Civilians. *Personal Justice Denied: Report of the Commission on Wartime Relocation and*

Sources

Internment of Civilians. Washington, D.C.: Civil Liberties Public Education Fund / Seattle: University of Washington Press, 1997.

Uyeda, Clifford. "A Change to 'Redress.'" *Pacific Citizen*, May 16, 1978, 47.

———. "Why Reparation?" *Pacific Citizen*, Oct. 28, 1977, 1.

Weglyn, Michi. *Years of Infamy: The Untold Story of America's Concentration Camps.* Seattle: University of Washington Press, [1976] 1995.

INDEX